Retire Early
Retire Wealthy

Your essential guide to Successful Property Investing

Roly Weaver

Retire Early Retire Wealthy

First published in 2013 by

Panoma Press
48 St Vincent Drive, St Albans, Herts, AL1 5SJ, UK

info@panomapress.com
www.panomapress.com

Book layout by Neil Coe

Printed on acid-free paper from managed forests. This
book is printed on demand to fulfill orders, so no copies
will be remaindered or pulped.

ISBN 978-1-908746-76-4

The right of Roly Weaver to be identified as the author of
this work has been asserted in accordance with sections 77
and 78 of the Copyright Designs and Patents Act 1988.

A CIP catalogue record for this book is available from the
British Library.

This book is available online and in all good bookstores.

What others say about this book

"Retire Early Retire Wealthy correctly identifies that individuals need to take control of their own financial future and provides numerous proven techniques to support the reader along this path. Everyone thinking about investing in property should read and grasp Roly's fundamental approach because it will lead to creating long term wealth. I know Roly is a caring, ethical and trustworthy person."

Steve Bolton, Founder of Platinum Property Partners

"With so many people realising their pension is unlikely to give them the income they need to lead the life they desire in retirement; 'Retire Early Retire Wealthy' provides lovely anecdotes, sound advice and proven strategies for money management and property investment. When followed, these techniques allow individuals to take control of their own financial future, and in-turn, their life! "

Juswant and Sylvia Rai, Founders and Hosts of Berkshire Property Meet

"From my 30 years experience in property I know that Roly's system works. Following Roly's methods, readers will be able to create a life of choice, and will be able to spend more time with their family and loved ones. Roly's recommendation and method – to become a professional armchair investor rather than managing everything yourself – is perfect if you don't want 'another job'; or simply don't have time."

Ian Clark, former Estate Agent as seen on TV, and Founder of Midas Estates

"Retire Early Retire Wealthy explains how to invest in property in a simple and clear, yet thorough way. Roly's straight forward approach clearly demonstrates his knowledge and expertise in the property investment arena. When you read this book you will wonder why you hadn't invested sooner. It may also re-invigorate your desire to continue investing. This is supported by practical methods that, when followed, will ensure you maximise the property's potential as well as your investment in order to achieve the best cashflow."

Dr. David Harwood, Property Mentor and Founder and Host of Exeter Property and Entrepreneur Network (PEN)

"Retire Early Retire Wealthy is jam-packed with vital; actionable information, that anybody serious about making a living through property needs to read. Learn from the expert. Roly will save you years of wasted time and pain; and more essentially, save you money, if you take note of his deep knowledge of property investing."

Greg and Fiona Scott, Authors of Living a Laptop Lifestyle

"After reading Roly's book I have rekindled my interest in investing in property. He explains the whole process in a sensible, reassuring way, and points out the possible pitfalls that may take an inexperienced investor by surprise. I think it is essential reading for anyone planning to embark on this venture".

Dana Finch, Project Manager, London

"Roly and Rachel have given me invaluable help purchasing my first buy-to-let flat, but their principles for life are also sound. This is not a get-rich-quick scheme but a doctrine to achieve your aim in life."

Commander Richard Coupe OBE, Civil & Commercial Mediator, Wellington, Somerset

"Roly is committed to transforming people's lives - he is constantly connecting people who he knows will be able help one another achieve their objectives, goals, ambitions and dreams. Roly's thorough and systemised approach to investing in property can be applied by anyone who has the audacity to map out a new vision and plan a positive future for themselves and their family."

Lee Cerio, Founder of Essential Living

"Through professional experience, comprehensive research and sound business management Roly and Rachel achieved their clear life changing objectives of freedom and financial independence. Now you can share their life changing secrets."

Pat Green, former colleague and Chartered Civil Engineer, Minehead

Acknowledgements

My journey to this point in time would not have been so exciting and fulfilling without the support from my wonderful wife, Rachel. You have been, and still are, many things to me; my loving, caring and considerate wife of 27 years; mother of our children; companion and friend; and diligent business partner. Thank you for your patience while I have been writing this book. I love you very much.

I am thankful for the support of my children; both now young adults with a lifetime ahead of them. You have given me so much joy and happiness and I look forward, with great excitement, to see where your paths lead you.

This book could not have been written if I had not started investing in property: so I would like to thank Tim who started me and Rachel on this path; and Jonathan, Neil R and Neil W who helped us purchase and manage our first few houses. Without knowing it, you all transformed our lives; we are so grateful.

Since I retired from my 'day job', I have met, and have been influenced by, so many fantastic people from various backgrounds: property colleagues; business owners; inspirational speakers; entrepreneurs; all of whom I owe a great debt to, for shaping my thoughts and giving me experiences that have led me to write this book. In particular, I thank Steve Bolton, Daniel Priestley and the KPI community for starting me off and actually making this book happen.

I also thank my friends and colleagues who reviewed my draft manuscripts and helped me to develop this book into what it is today. In particular, my thanks go to Lee and Gervaise Cerio, Francis and Jane Dolley and John Cato for your help in giving me direction from time to time. You all provided great insights, encouragement and added value – brilliant.

I want to say thank you Sreejith from yiking labs, elance, email: yiking-gizmo@yahoo.in for designing and producing my illustrations – I love them.

Finally, my life would not be so rich without the love, support, experiences and encouragement that I have had from my Mum and Dad. Thank you.

Contents

Preface:

Let me introduce myself – my story in brief

Welcome to my book *Retire Early Retire Wealthy*. I am Roly Weaver.

Well, it's your book really – if you want to increase your income, your understanding of wealth through successful property investment and have a wonderful life for yourself, then this book is for you. I want to help change your life. I want to help you to *Retire Early Retire Wealthy*.

Why am I so confident that you will be able to transform your life? Not just your finances, but your life?

The answer to that is simple.

Together with my wife, Rachel, I started investing in UK property in March 2002. Just 6 years later, in March 2008 at the age of 50, I was able to fulfil my long-standing dream to *retire early. My life changed.*

In fact my life had begun to change shortly after buying our first property because it suddenly dawned on me that investing in property had the potential to be my retirement plan. Well, it sure turned out to be that. I am so grateful.

Once I began to realize how it was changing my life, I felt inspired, liberated and in control of my own destiny. I am sure you will feel this way too.

After our first couple of purchases, I felt that my job was now a 'means to an end' rather than a job with no end. Even my colleagues at work began asking me why I was smiling so much. I didn't tell them why until the day I decided to quit.

Most people don't become financially free.

My view of financial freedom is not having to work for a living; to be able to live a lifestyle of my choice where my investments and savings are generating all the money I need.

Looking back now, I don't think I even thought about becoming financially free when I used to work for a living. The concept never entered my head. I had a job, and then I would retire on a pension. I expected my pension to give me sufficient income to support my desired lifestyle. That is what I was taught. Also the term 'financially free' implied that one had to be rich, with the underlying connotations that many people feel about 'being rich'. I now know that 'rich' is very subjective and everyone has a different view of what 'rich' means. So I have learnt that 'financially free' is a much better term. This can be defined by each person in their own way.

How it used to be for me

My experience at work was that I never once heard colleagues talking about retiring early. In fact, we were so wrapped up in working hard to do a good job, to please our boss in order to get a pay-rise or promotion - that we hardly had time for anything else except to work. Even thinking about changing jobs took a back seat in my mind - until I had finally had enough.

I could not see how I could afford some of the luxuries I desired and also, I was worried about my retirement because my pension was not going to give me the lifestyle I currently had, let alone the one I wanted. I would have to work longer, possibly downsize my home and restrict my life to match the income I would receive. Discussions were along the lines of; 'I need to work longer'; 'I cannot afford to give up work'.

At that time I was generally frustrated at work because...

- There was way too much work to do.

- There was continual political interference and bureaucracy.

- I didn't have enough money to pay for **ALL** the things I wanted - like going away more often and generally enjoying activities outside work.

- I wished there was more time to spend with family and friends; time for myself and time to support other people or charities.

- **AND** I would have preferred a little less pressure at work!

- I hated not being able to get on in my job more quickly, to attain higher status and salary

- I hated not being in control of my financial future.

 I secretly feared that my job was no longer secure and that I could be made redundant at any time without much prospect of getting another job.

DO YOU HAVE SIMILAR FRUSTRATIONS?

I changed my approach in order to get a different result

Once I realized that I needed more money to support my children going to University, I knew something had to change. My job was not going to give me the money I needed.

I was given the idea of investing in property by my local estate agent. Rachel and I have never looked back since. We built a property portfolio that generated more income than I was earning in my job as a Chartered Civil Engineer. We had become financially free: meaning that the income generated from our properties exceeded the amount of money we needed to live on.

I now have time for my family; time to help other people in need and support worthwhile organizations. For example, Rachel and I are Patrons of Peace One Day (www. peaceoneday.org). Please read more about this at the end of this book.

I am very grateful that I started investing in property and began my journey to financial freedom.

I want to be known for helping transform people's lives. And I would love to be able to help you transform your life. We were never taught how to manage money, let alone how to create sufficient wealth for ourselves. This means we have become dependent on other people to provide for us. We work long hours if we have a job and then rely on pensions to give us enough money to live once we stop work. Jobs are no longer for life and pensions generally don't give us the income that we need to enjoy our retirement.

I have found that when I started to gain control of my finances, the rest of my life followed. I would like to share with you how I did this so that you can see it is possible for you too. I get so much joy from helping people to succeed and in this book I provide ideas and practical tools to help you *Retire Early Retire Wealthy* and minimise the risk of making mistakes.

My original intention was to write a book about UK property investing. I soon realized, however, that the knowledge I gained on my journey is of significant benefit to many people, not just those who decide that investing in UK property is their desired path to financial security. So this book has become more than just teaching you about property investment.

Retire Early Retire Wealthy gives you the opportunity to:

- Review how you think about money and why it is important

- Manage your money so that you gain control of your finances, allowing you to invest into assets, knowing that an asset puts money in your pocket rather than taking it out

- Learn that by investing in a professional way, the UK property market can help you become financially independent

- Learn how to do this safely, thereby avoiding many of the pitfalls awaiting unwary investors

- Work with other people, knowing you are not alone

- Create the life you desire, that is recession-proof.

This is supported by my educational workshops and on-line education material.

By taking focused action after reading this book, I am convinced your life will never be the same again. *You can*

Retire Early Retire Wealthy. If you make the choice, within 6 – 14 years you have the real potential to sack your boss, just as I did and *Retire Early.* You may even be able to achieve this sooner, but this will depend upon your own circumstances.

Isn't that a wonderful thought?

To your success,

Roly

Introduction:

What this book can do for you

Investing in UK property helped me to retire early. My salary was replaced by the income from my property portfolio. *Retire Early Retire Wealthy* will show you how I managed to do this.

The property experience

When you follow the guidelines, rules and processes explained in this book, I know that you will be in a position to make these life-changing choices yourself. This is not a 'get-rich-quick' scheme, but it is a reliable and secure way to see your wealth increase to new levels, providing you do this professionally.

Retire Early Retire Wealthy therefore gives you a massive advantage over where my wife, Rachel, and I started; we had to learn how to go about this for ourselves and we did this without any training or reading of books. We developed our own understanding of the rules needed to succeed, developed our own systems and worked out where and when to buy. I believe I was able to do this by applying the skills and knowledge I learnt from my professional career as a Chartered Civil Engineer.

By following my methods and processes to invest in UK property, you will save yourself a significant amount of your time and your money. You will learn the fundamentals of property investing and specifically how to:

- buy the *right property in the right location at the right price*

- buy property below surveyed value
- add value to the property
- avoid the pitfalls that many other investors stumble into
- use the systems I have developed

You will be able to do this from the comfort of your own home, if you so wish, but only once you have learnt the fundamentals.

Life changing moments

There are times in life when something happens to make us change our course, our journey through life. I have found, through my life and speaking with others that, in the main, this occurs because of some pain that has happened, or is imminent. The life changing moment is rarely caused by the thought of joy and happiness pulling us towards a particular path. We are good at reacting to events but not so good at pro-actively planning for our own benefit.

Our subconscious mind is designed to protect us and keep us safe. What we do right now is safe. We know what the outcomes of our current actions are likely to be. Our mind protects us, by getting us to think that the consequences of any new actions will be difficult, unhelpful, and painful. So we don't go there; we don't like change.

· · · · ·

"Doing the same thing over and over again and expecting different outcome"

Einstein's definition of insanity!

· · · · ·

My vision is to help you to *Retire Early Retire Wealthy*, so I urge you to open up your mind *now*, to the possibility that you could become financially free. It *will* happen - if you follow a well designed plan. Do not wait for the pain to kick in. Maybe just take a moment to consider whether your pension is guaranteed to generate a comfortable lifestyle for you, or will you have to down-size and live a restricted, careful life?

Our world is changing and to many of us it seems that we no longer control our own lives: our pension plans are unlikely to provide the income we need; our jobs are no longer secure; our salary is being overtaken by inflation; reductions in our state benefits and medical support potentially puts our future in turmoil and getting on the property ladder is harder than ever.

Why did you pick up this book?

I have heard many stories about people who have had a traumatic experience in their life; suicide attempts; living on the streets; drug addiction; massive disability and more. They had to make a choice for their survival. Do they accept their position and their heartache and misery, or do they get on and do something positive with their lives?

A lot of the successful people I have met have had some serious misfortune in their life. Once they realized the position they were in, or had come through, they used this as a driver to succeed and decided to make something positive happen. They became focused on making sure that this would not happen again. They have managed to turn their lives around and became very successful in their chosen field.

Rachel and I are extremely fortunate that nothing like this

happened to us or our families. However, our kick start was the moment we considered our future and realized that we did not have a way of fulfilling our future needs and desires. This became our focus over several months, trying to work out to how to obtain the money we needed. By focusing on our goal and talking to people about it, we came across property investing.

Do not wait for an external kick start. Do not wait until you realize you need the extra cash. Do not wait until an unfortunate event befalls you. Why not start to create your life today?

To change the way we think about money, we need a WHY. Why would you want more money? What would be its purpose? If the purpose is great enough and strong enough, it will give you a passion to make it happen.

Once you have found your Why, you become committed to making it happen. Then anything is possible. Although I am talking about money specifically, it is not really about the money. It is what money can do, that really counts.

Just consider for a moment why did you pick up this book? I hope it was the title that inspired you – with the underlying implication that this book will change your life. So why do you want your life to change?

What is your Why?

I have received many different answers to this question. I hate my job; I haven't got enough money; I don't have time for my family and loved ones; I can't live on my pension – I have to continue working. In all cases people wanted to change their current situation so that they could be in control of their own future.

Retire Early Retire Wealthy is designed to help. You will learn:

- Why you need to create your life starting today
- How wealth is created
- Why investing in UK property professionally provides cash in your hand and long-term wealth
- There is a more profitable way of life than exchanging your time for money
- Why you should only buy property in Roly's Golden Zone
- How Roly's Property Analyser minimises your property investment risk
- What you need to account for when you give up employment
- How to gain control of your finances – so the rest of your life can follow
- How to build your freedom investment fund
- How to leverage other people's time, money and expertise

The important thing is to take targeted action, now, otherwise nothing changes.

You need to decide your life goals and dreams. Then create a plan on how to get there and set measurable specific targets so that you know you have achieved them.

Don't forget to celebrate your successes along the way!

Retire Early Retire Wealthy helps you to set out your plan because:

· · · · ·

"If you don't design your own life plan, chances are you'll fall into someone else's plan!

And guess what they have planned for you? Nothing much."

Jim Rohn, 1930 to 2009, was an American business philosopher who taught people to focus on the fundamentals of human behaviour that most affected personal and business performance.

· · · · ·

Property investment can work for you

People enjoy being involved in property investment: some see it as a way to become financially free; others see it as a way to focus their mind on something positive; an introduction to new friends; or a way to join other people in a world outside their current environment. However, everyone gets pleasure out of the returns property investing can make. You can start investing if you have some savings. You can even start if you only have a little money because you can enter into a 'joint venture' with others to make it work.

Property investment can work for you if you have a well paid job, are self-employed; a small business owner or unemployed. There are sufficient opportunities for everyone. This book will even help you if you are looking to purchase your own home, as it will shed new light on the way you can manage your money, think about property and the way you look at assets and liabilities.

Some people make property investment their full time job and some do this alongside their regular job, but many are professional 'armchair' investors who let others help them achieve their goals.

You may have built up a pot of money already; or perhaps you have recently acquired it. Now you wish to make that money work for you, rather than let it dwindle away or reduce in value by keeping it in a bank or low-paying savings plan.

If you feel that you don't have enough money to start investing in property at this time, this book will teach you the strategies. It will give you the ideas to help you to become financially aware and the opportunities to work with other people and property experts.

Once you have read *Retire Early Retire Wealthy* I know you will be inspired; liberated and in a position to gain control of your life. Your mind will have expanded to see what is possible and you will be open to new opportunities and expectations.

You will realize that your dreams can become your reality.

The most important thing is that you take action otherwise nothing will change

So have fun and be prepared to Retire Early Retire Wealthy

Notes for readers – supporting resources

Links to useful websites

In this book I provide you with useful website addresses, but I recognise over time, that some of these addresses may change. I have therefore decided to maintain an up-to-date list on my website.

Exercise templates

I strongly recommend that you complete the exercises I have set out so that you can gain the full benefit of this book.

For some of these exercises, I have created templates that you can use. You can download these from my website rather than having to create your own.

Recommended reading

The books I mention in *Retire Early Retire Wealthy* are listed under the 'recommended reading' section of the 'resources' page of my website.

What to look for in this book

When you see 'Happy Jim with his laptop' you will know that there are resources available to you on my website.

My website 'Resources' page, where I manage all links to the useful websites, the exercise templates and the recommended reading list, is http://mylifesolutions.co.uk/education/resources/

This QR code will also take you there.

PART I
Expanding your dreams

· · · · ·

"If you can imagine it, you can achieve it;
if you can dream it, you can become it"

William Arthur Ward (1921 – 1994), one of America's most
quoted writers of inspirational maxims

· · · · ·

CHAPTER 1
A journey to financial freedom

I am glad that you have found this book, it is packed with information, stories and insights that will enable you to *Retire Early Retire Wealthy* and I am sure it will change your life forever.

It is based on the journey that I have had with my wife, Rachel; from when we started to invest in property in March 2002 until today. An important stage for us along the way was when I retired from my 'day' job on 31st March 2008: just 6 years after buying our first buy-to-let property.

Through the returns on our investments, we can now do what we choose to do; with whom we want and when we want. We create the rules of our life. If you are in control of the rules – how can you lose?

A brief look at how the journey worked for us

Rachel and I both had regular jobs for the majority of our lives. I am a Chartered Civil Engineer and have worked for a variety of organizations and companies. Rachel had various part-time jobs to help top-up my salary so we could afford to live a reasonable lifestyle and go on holidays. Our children went to local schools, played various sports and joined local clubs such as swimming, trampolining and scouting. As you can imagine, all this needed to be paid for.

Whilst at work, I never really got a chance to think about much outside work. During 2001, when I was 44 years old, Rachel and I came to the conclusion that my job was not really supporting our desired lifestyle. We loved our holidays and that's where we spent all our spare cash. When we came to look further at our longer term needs, we realized that we would not easily be able to support our children going to University and then later, possibly getting married. And I had always wanted to retire early! Looking at our income and expenses, we were hardly keeping our heads above water; let alone able to afford to pay for these large future lump sums. How could we afford these things?

Without realising it at the time, we had set our subconscious minds to work!

The creative mind at work

I guess I have always been quite an optimist and so thinking positively was not difficult for me. Nevertheless, I could not fathom out what we should do, but I knew we had to do something. I now believe my subconscious was 'on the lookout' for me. In October 2001, we had a letter in the post offering a free financial assessment. We wouldn't normally bother with these things, but on this occasion we made an arrangement for someone to call at our house the following month.

The assessment showed us that we could remortgage our home and take out an increased mortgage, giving us around £60,000 in our pockets. The interest rates were lower than we were paying at that time, so it would not cost much more each month to finance the additional borrowing. Never, until that moment, had the notion of borrowing money from our home occurred to us. We knew intuitively that we should not just put this money in the bank; we knew we had to put this money to work in order to create additional income.

The thought of taking on a loan for the purposes of investing was nerve-wracking. We had never been taught what to invest in, or what the investment process consisted of. I was afraid that if we took the extra money and could not find something profitable to do with it, we would start to lose the little savings we did have and we would have to cut back on some of the things we enjoyed doing. How would we be able to pay back the loan?

We took another month to decide that we would take action and remortgage, even though we had no idea what we would do with the money. This was a big risk but we decided to do it anyway. The need and desire to find the extra cash to pay for our children's future was more of an incentive than to sit back and do nothing. We had a drive and an inclination that we would find something to do with it; something that would generate us some extra money.

When I was young, my mum and dad had bought two caravans and put them on a site near Weymouth. I remember they always seemed to be changing the bed linen each week, so I guess they must have had a successful little business. I suggested to Rachel that we should look into buying a caravan or two and rent them out. We didn't do much more at that stage.

The light bulb moment

In January 2002, I was in the gym; not that I enjoyed going but I thought it might do me some good after the Christmas indulgences!

I had seen this guy a couple of times, whom I recognised as the local estate agent that we had bought our house from in summer 2000. Anyway, I got chatting to him and I mentioned about the caravans. He suggested I consider buying a house and renting that out instead. Property would rise in value (appreciate) but a caravan would lose value (depreciate). He told me to call in at his office to look at some property details.

I wonder?

He spent some time with me telling me how it could work and pointed me in the direction of the local letting agent. Both were very helpful, providing me with valuable information and various possibilities. After a couple of weeks looking for suitable properties via estate agents, I met an excellent Independent Financial Advisor (IFA). He showed me how buy-to-let mortgages worked and gave me some ideas to work through. Rachel and I analysed all this newly found knowledge at home over the next few weeks.

We discovered that 'the numbers' seem to work out. We found we could buy a house, take out a buy-to-let mortgage, rent it out and have more money coming in - than we would spend on the mortgage, insurance, anticipated expenses etc.

In March 2002, we agreed to buy our first buy-to-let property. Not that we knew it at the time, but we had begun to understand the first few of steps of the property investment process. More about this in Chapter 8.

The first 3 steps of the property investing process

We relied upon local people to provide guidance in this strange new world. We needn't have worried because they proved to be fantastic in their particular area of expertise:

estate agent; letting agent; solicitor and financial advisor. Our problem was to work out how to fit it all together. They all gave their opinions and advice but ultimately, I had to make the final decision which house to buy; which mortgage product to use; what type of tenants I wanted; etc. Although finding and managing our properties was time consuming and hard work in the beginning, I was able to use my professional skills as a Chartered Civil Engineer to fathom out how to create effective and efficient systems of work. In my job, I was used to assessing risk and putting contingency plans into place. I believe this helped me design my robust systems for investing in property in a secure way. I share my property investing experiences with you in this book so you can appreciate that this can work for you as well. You can follow my tried and tested systems.

Over time Rachel and I have been learning more and more. Our systems, processes, money management and overall expertise have helped us to develop this very profitable and successful business. The steps that you will learn about in *Retire Early Retire Wealthy* have improved since our early days – so you will have the benefit of all our skills and experience when you embark upon *your* journey.

By May 2006 we had a portfolio of properties.

On the 31st March 2008 aged 50, I retired from my day job.

How the journey could work for you

Our systems and analysis have protected us from many of the pitfalls that some 'would-be' property investors encounter. We developed these from working out the fundamental basics for ourselves. We did not have any 'property training' and this meant that we taught ourselves everything. We had to find out how and why 'the numbers worked'. We did not have anyone to teach us their methods. The outcome is that we developed a system that did not cut corners or make inappropriate assumptions. We became professional.

A 'professional' investor learns the fundamental skills to make the right investment decisions, whereas a 'would-be' investor may not necessarily know that they have missed out on essential knowledge. They often jump into the process half way through; for example, not learning which would be the right property to buy to ensure it produces regular long term income.

Between the time we started in 2002 and the time I retired in 2008, Rachel was doing the majority of the day-to-day property management whilst I was at work. When I got home, we spent time reviewing our finances; carrying out physical maintenance on the houses; looking for our next

purchases and refinancing our existing mortgages. I was effectively undertaking two jobs – my regular job and managing the buy-to-let portfolio.

If holding down two jobs is not for you, then I would recommend taking a completely passive approach to this by asking someone else, whom you know and trust, to guide you and support you. You will then be provided with the comfort, support and expert guidance that you need to ensure that your journey to *Retire Early Retire Wealthy* is joyful and less stressful than it would otherwise be.

If you do not own property at the moment, don't worry. You will learn how you can begin to gain control of your life and set yourself up for the financial independence you desire. For example, at the time of writing, you do not need to own your own property to obtain a buy-to-let mortgage. How fantastic is that!

An eye-opener for me was that prior to this break through moment, in all the time that I had been employed, I had never once thought of improving my financial position in any way other than working longer and harder at my job.

I now realize that many people still have this mind-set. I want to help you to consider your job 'as a means to an end' rather than 'a job with no end'. By embarking upon this journey you will be able to enjoy your job much more. I did.

> A few months after we bought our first couple of properties, I realized that my job was helping me to retire. I began to feel in control, *I had begun to create my own life.* My colleagues started asking me why I was always smiling. I just said that I enjoyed my job, because that is how I felt. I did not tell them, however, that I had begun my journey to financial freedom.

Like many people, I have become disillusioned with pension products, waiting for others to invest my money and hoping that they make the right decision. This book will show you an alternative way for you to create your own pension. If you have a pension plan at the moment, it may be possible to use this fund to buy residential UK property.

Top Tip Investing in UK property professionally is safe and your long term wealth is assured, as long as you do it correctly. Do not cut corners. This is not a get-rich-quick scheme.

Put into practice what you learn.

Take targeted action.

CHAPTER 2
Creating wealth

Our upbringing

When we are young we are told to save money, generally in a bank or building society. These savings will be used to pay for those special events: Christmas presents or a holiday maybe and also, to pay for the unexpected, such as replacing the fridge or getting the car back on the road.

We are not told to invest in our future. We are told to invest in a pension. Traditional pensions work some of the time – but during the economic climate of 2008 to 2012, we see that the financial institutions are reducing the pension pay-out because they have not been able to invest the money that we gave them very well. Many of the jobs in local councils and other organizations are changing from a 'final salary' (defined benefit) pension scheme to one which requires an employee to put in a specific contribution each month but with no guarantee of the 'output' (i.e. their pension) at the end (defined contribution).

In the main, I have found that much of the advice given about savings and retirement plans does not result in very good returns for us as individuals.

Bank and building society saving accounts do not give a good return on your money either.

I have also noticed in 2011 and 2012 significant changes to the world we live in:

- Major banks, countries and the monetary system have been collapsing
- Pensions are no longer guaranteed to give us a secure future
- Welfare benefits are being cut
- Jobs are no longer for life
- Credit is difficult to get

Top Tip We need to change the way we think and act. We need to concentrate on getting our own house in order and stop relying on others.

Our world is changing.

- "UK banks receive £37bn bail-out" BBC 13 Oct 2008

- "2008 UK bank rescue package totalling some £500bn was announced by the British Government on 8th Oct 2008" Wikipedia

- "Barclays' widening Libor-fixing scandal" BBC 17 July 2012

- "Fitch says Spanish banking bailout may not suffice" The Economic Times 10th Aug 2012

- "Standard Chartered (Bank) Prepares for Iran Money Laundering Hearing" International Business Times 13th Aug 2012

HOW PAYOUTS HAVE NOSEDIVED'

	2007	PENSION Today	Change %
Britannic (1)	£8,786	£3,861	-56.1
Britannia Life (1)	£6,546	£3,643	-44.4
Prudential	£8,197	£4,614	-43.7
Norwich Union (2)	£6,602	£3,752	-43.2
National Provident Life (1)	£6,427	£3,701	-42.4
Legal & General	£6,478	£3,897	-39.8
Scottish Provident (1)	£7,375	£4,444	-39.7
Scottish Widows	£5,979	£3,676	-38.5
Pearl (1)	£6,027	£3,752	-37.8
Scottish Amicable	£7,740	£4,883	-36.9
Scottish Mutual (1)	£6,646	£4,239	-36.2
General Accident (2)	£6,819	£4,443	-34.8
Friends Provident (3)	£6,292	£4,148	-34.1
Life Association of Scotland (1)	£7,187	£4,840	-32.6
Royal Life (1)	£6,535	£4,418	-32.4
London Life (1)	£5,140	£3,685	-28.3
Standard Life	£5,708	£4,117	-27.9
Sun Life (3)	£6,927	£5,015	-27.6
Axa Sun Life (3)	£6,489	£5,212	-19.7

'Based on a £200 a month 20-year policy for man retiring at 65 on current annuity rates
(1) Part of the Phoenix Group (2) Part of Aviva (3) Part of Friends Life

Pensions take a nose dive

Source "This is Money - Feb 29th 2012"

"The sick cost of cuts to benefits – seriously ill losing out on vital funds"

"Homeowners forced to free up equity during retirement"

NHS 'cannot afford' £2 billion elderly care

NHS leaders will today warn ministers that the health service does not have the cash to pay the £2 billion a year shortfall in funding for elderly care. The NHS Confederation says the Treasury must urgently come up with the money to avoid a crisis. David Rogers, Chairman of the LGA's Community Wellbeing Board, said: "As resources become increasingly stretched, closer and more effective working between councils and the NHS will be an essential part of how we look after our ageing population. However, there is unquestionably an immediate and growing funding crisis in adult social care which needs to be urgently addressed, alongside wider reform to the system to make it simpler and fairer."

Local government Assoc. Daily News Headlines 24 September 2012

'The social care system has been under-funded for years, failing to keep pace with the rising demand of an ageing population,'

Michelle Mitchell, charity director at Age UK

Jobs are no longer for life

According to research amongst workers carried out by Office Angels, a leading office recruitment agency.

The concept of 'a career – let alone a job - for life' could have all but disappeared within 25 years, replaced by workers pursuing a succession of different career paths and even "multi-jobbing".

A study by the Association of Accounting Technicians (the professional body for accounting technicians) concludes that a job is no longer for life. Their findings:

- One in four Brits are bored of their job and desperate to leave.

- A study into the job satisfaction of 2,000 people revealed three quarters had ended up in a career they hadn't intended on.

- Rather than display loyalty to their current place of work, most take a 'fend for yourself' approach and plan to leave their current job within five years.

- In fact, the 'job for life' mentality is dead - with only one in three employees planning to commit themselves to their current place of work long term.

Very few jobs are for life. I believe the working world has changed and people, especially young people, should not expect a job for life. People either need to become highly skilled and keep acquiring more skills to enable them to adapt to the changing marketplace or they need to build their own safety net and become less dependent on the salary generated by their working income. The world is becoming more entrepreneurial.

It is becoming harder to get personal credit, according to new research.

The Centre for Economics and Business Research says 2.3 million Brits have been turned down for a credit card or unsecured loan in the last six months.

It's simply the fact that lending institutions have become much more strict," Paul Lewis, Vice President of Credit Confidential tells the Wake Up To Money programme, "in terms of who they're happy to lend money to."

BBC News, 18 April 2011

What this means to us:

- Paper money is not worth much and we don't know what it will be worth in the future so we need to hold our wealth in assets
- We need to understand how to manage money, credit and debt
- We cannot rely on the Government to fully support us in retirement
- Pension providers cannot tell us with any certainty what they will give us
- We will need to keep contributing more and more to our pensions to ensure we get something reasonable back
- We need to gain control of our pension provision ourselves

- We need to go back to a bartering system where like minded people work in collaboration and joint venture to support each other's services and products in order to create our own real wealth

So what do the wealthy people do?

How do people become wealthy? Many of the wealthy people started with very little – so it is not to do with 'they started from a better position' than us.

Let me talk generally for a moment about successful people. This goes beyond money.

A lot of their success is down to having a vision; a 'can-do' attitude; a focused mind and a system. Whilst it may appear they have luck, I believe it is actually the way they think and act that gives positive results.

For example, successful people have the same amount of time; the same economy; the same environment; the same seasons; the same ... everything as everyone else. So what is different?

It is said that an individual's wealth is the average of the 5 people they spend most of their time with. You can see this happening when sports athletes or footballers get together. Their attitude to win rubs off on each other and success breeds success. Like-minded successful people work together to promote ideas and give support. Unsuccessful people seem to moan about ... well almost everything, and get support from those who are there to listen.

Let us briefly have a look at the way successful people face everyday issues. The wonderful; inspiring young entrepreneur, Daniel Priestley, suggests:

What regular people say (not you of course!)	And what successful people say
I'm here to do a good job	I'm here to get results
I'm not good enough	But I will get it done anyway
It has to be perfect or I won't start	It has to be great and I'm going to improve things
When it's perfect I will start talking to people	I will talk to people today
My voice sounds funny	Me too, so I will just hope it's a remarkable selling feature
I've never done this before	I'm doing this for the first time ... how exciting
I'm embarrassed in front of the camera	So I will remember it's not about me
I don't have something I need, so I will stop	I will get what I need, whatever it is
I need more support	I need to co-create a supportive environment by supporting others
I'm focussed on learning	I'm focussed on producing
Whatever I'm told	Whatever it takes
And my statement: I'm so busy, I have no time	I have the same 24 hours as everyone else. Until I gain control of my life, my job is to become good at property investing

Do you recognise any of these statements when you listen to people around you?

When I talk about successful people, I am thinking of wealthy people and wealth can be measured in many ways:

- health
- relationships
- home
- work
- personality
- finance

It is a reflection of the way you view your life now and how you wish it to be in the future.

Successful people learn skills and take action

Successful people decide what they would like to achieve and work out how to make it happen. If new skills are needed, they either learn from people that are already successful in that arena, or employ them. Once the method of execution is known, they take the vitally important step: **take action.**

In the context of property investment, some of the key skills are:

Leverage

Leverage is about utilising tools other than the ones you alone possess (or wish to use), that, when employed alongside the tools you do have, produce an outcome that you could not have achieved on your own - hopefully for your benefit.

People in the UK financial sector often use the term 'gearing' instead of leverage. Gearing is about borrowing money, say in the form of a loan or mortgage, and using that money to generate an income greater than the interest you pay for the loan. This requires earning a 'rate of return' on the money employed greater than the loan interest rate. The money loaned can be used to purchase assets that generate income, or be used to invest in a business, with the expectation that the business will generate income. The business borrowing the money will undertake a risk assessment to evaluate the likelihood of making and losing money on this venture. Money is the tool in this case.

In a mechanical sense, gears on a bicycle allow you to generate more speed with the same amount of effort. When you peddle along in a 'small' gear, it helps you to start off and to climb hills more easily. If you want to go faster, you use the 'larger' gears. The effort you put in is multiplied by the use of gears. You are leveraging the physical gear size to generate more speed with the same energy.

Taking this a stage further, gears are used to lift heavy loads using the same effort. In this case, the gears are more commonly called pulleys. Pull on the chain passing over a small pulley, then over a slightly larger one and so on, will produce a lot of leverage so you can lift heavier objects than you could if you are unaided.

The term 'leverage' though goes beyond the normally accept UK term of gearing. Leverage is about using what someone else has got, to your advantage. So now we can expand this to include 'other peoples' time'; 'other peoples' knowledge'; 'other peoples' skills'; 'other peoples' business' etc.

Understanding the power of leverage

Let us look at several ways to use leverage. These involve utilising other peoples':

- Money
- Time
- Knowledge and skills

Money

We borrow money from a bank or lender. We invest that money into property. Property does two things for us. It generates more income than it costs us to pay back the interest on the loan, i.e. it provides positive cash flow. Also, the property value goes up over time and we keep the increase in value for ourselves. I explain this in more detail in later chapters. Providing you follow my rules, you should not have to sell your investment property. This means that even when property values go down from time to time, negative equity does not become an issue. It only becomes a loss if you decide to sell your property.

Time

Although I am teaching you the fundamentals of money management and property investment in this book, it can be quite time consuming if you decide to do it all yourself. It becomes another job. At the beginning Rachel and I did not mind, mainly because we did not realize there was another way and also we were used to working hard. We thought that we had to work hard to get extra money. That was what we were taught; work hard and get a good job.

Now we realize that that statement is NOT entirely true. We can work SMART and make a good income. This has meant that we arrange for people to do jobs that free up our time. This means we can spend more time together, with family, with friends, taking holidays and thinking of new things to do.

We still manage a few of our properties ourselves on a day to day basis. I can't get out of the habit! However, we have begun to use tradesmen more and more for jobs I could do myself. We don't mind paying for these services because 'time' is sometimes more important to us than 'money'.

There are people, such as myself, and organizations that can help with property education and the investment process. Their services will significantly reduce the amount of time you need to spend yourself (Chapter 6) on learning this from scratch.

Knowledge and skills

Using other people's knowledge and skills is a little like making use of other people's time. The difference is, of course, that they have a particular skill built up through formal education and training and/or years of specific experience. They have become very accomplished at what they do.

It would be difficult for you and me to be as good as them within a short space of time. So the question you have to ask yourself is whether it is worth you taking months or years to learn a new skill or whether you pay someone to do this for you.

Think of Richard Branson; he has ideas and then he employs others to take them forward. He reaps the benefits of their skills.

I don't think I want to be a lawyer or an accountant. But I do want to understand the fundamentals of what they do – so I can monitor what they do; ensure they do a good job for me etc.

Within property investing there are many niches in which to make a living or obtain great investments. There are so many that I do not care to learn them all. But I know about them and I know who to ask if I need to.

You need to find an investment area that you feel comfortable with. Find an expert in that field and work with them. I am great at buy-to-let and adding value to properties. My specific skill is analysing numbers; setting up robust systems and checks and managing risk. This is what I call 'the fundamentals'.

In fact I believe you need to learn the fundamentals BEFORE you learn any other aspect of property investing. This is why I teach this at my workshops around the country.

My strong suggestion is to understand the fundamentals of property investment and then use professionals and experts in the specific niche you want to invest in.

 Using skilful people also means that you won't make costly mistakes.

Another useful learning point here is that you should not listen or take advice from anyone who is not qualified or who has not been successful already. For example, many people have a view on the property market. And why not? They live in or own a property. They read what they see in the newspaper and hear reports on the television. But here's the thing, most people that write articles or report in the media, are not professional landlords. They have not been taught how property investment works. They obtain information from analysts, who themselves are making a point that supports their company's stance.

Working together

You may be a little afraid of pursuing these ideas on your own. You may not have all the skills necessary. You may not have any start-up money. You may simply need someone to bounce ideas off.

 What everyone needs is a mentor, but not just any mentor. They must complement the skills and desires that you have. They must be experienced and have accomplished the things you want to pursue. I am suggesting that a community of like-minded people enjoy sharing knowledge and working together, forming Joint Ventures.

They are unlikely to be your friend down the pub who just talks a lot, or has a view because they have 'read it in the papers'.

In addition to providing education, I also offer mentoring in wealth creation, property investment and money management.

Top Tip Do not listen or take advice from friends down the pub or club; or from the media.

Listen and learn from the experts.

Property is working for our children

Our teenage children were each given £1000 by their grandparents in 2003. We suggested that they could use the money to buy a house with us and they agreed. Their £1000 equated to 5% of the money needed for the deposit and purchase costs. In 2006 we refinanced the house to buy another and they ended up with a further 3% in the new house.

By 2011, their £1000 has grown to be worth £2035 and they have already received £1201 cash from the net rental profit. How cool is that?

Our children leveraged my time and knowledge, and we all leveraged the banks' money! We worked together to make this a success for us and we invested in an asset that put money in our pockets. Maybe this idea could work for you.

Top Tip If you have not got much money to start with, look to work with someone else at the beginning. This is called a Joint Venture (JV).

Investing in assets

Most people are not very good at investing in assets. BUT this is the real essence of gaining control of your finances. This is the ONLY way it will work. We must invest in assets to be properly in control.

An asset is simply something that puts money in your pocket. If you buy something that costs you money each month, then this is a liability. Even if this cost is depreciation: a car is therefore, counter-intuitively, a liability and not an asset.

Once you begin to buy assets, then the income will flow to you on a regular basis. The value of the investment will grow. If you can achieve this without working full time at it, then this is passive income, because you don't have to do too much to keep that money coming in. You now have time to look for another asset to invest your money in.

Creating an investment pot

In order to be able to purchase an asset you will need to find ways to create a pot of money to start your investment process. I am specifically asking you to create an investment pot. Not a general savings plan for, say, a holiday or a car. Ideally you should be looking to invest around 10% of your income. Sounds a lot doesn't it? Well, you can start smaller and gradually grow towards it.

• • • • •

"A little of what I earn I keep"

The Richest Man in Babylon (see more below)

• • • • •

George Clason, an American businessman and writer (1874-1957) best known for writing information pamphlets about being thrifty and how to achieve financial success which were issued by banks and insurance companies, compiled his work into an all-time motivational classic, 'The Richest Man in Babylon'. In this he tells of Arkad, a man of humble origins, who 'becomes' the Richest Man in Babylon by keeping a portion of his income for himself and investing it wisely.

He suggests the amount you keep should not be less than 10% of your earnings; invest it wisely, based upon good advice from an expert; then re-invest the income from those savings. Year on year you will have the benefit of compounding growth.

Just think about this for a moment. Most people spend all of their income, no matter how much that is. George Clason is saying that we need to change that habit and put the first portion away for **US**, no-one else! We need to build an investment pot.

Top Tip The idea here is that the first person you pay is YOURSELF. Get into this habit today.

If you already contribute to investment plans or additional pension contributions, that's great. You can start with these. In some cases it is now possible to use money from your current pension fund to buy UK property. WOW !

If you are not saving at the moment for your long term future, then you need to start now. Please don't say, 'I don't have enough money to start with'. If you are serious about creating an abundant life for yourself and your family, you need to start investing now. Even if it is only a £1 a week, say £5 per month. It may be difficult at first but you will get used to it.

Rachel and I have come to appreciate how this method of allocating funds is absolutely crucial if you want to have more financial freedom ... *and* stay there. I say more about this in Chapter 10.

Top Tip NEVER SPEND YOUR INVESTMENT POT ... because ...

It will eventually provide you with a passive income more than you need. Then, and only then, can you start to spend the generated income - if you choose to

Becoming wealthy

I have intimated that you need to invest in assets to be wealthy. This is made clear by Robert Kiyosaki, an American investor, businessman and author, in his book 'Rich Dad, Poor Dad'. He describes four person profiles.

Two profiles are of an employee and a self-employed person. In these profiles you are paid wages. You pay your bills and spend the remainder of the money you have on other necessities of life. Some is saved in a bank etc. In a nutshell you are exchanging your time for money; even the investments you are generally advised to take, hardly cover the rate of inflation.

The other two profiles are of someone who either owns their own business or is an investor that has assets that have significant growth. Owning a business differs from being self employed in that the business will continue to run and produce an income when you are not working in it. A self-employed business or a small business that requires you to be there most of the time falls into the self-employed profile. The business owner and investor have assets that are providing growth well above inflation.

Plan to be a business owner; an investor or both. This is where you want to end up because this is where your income is made without you having to do much at all, i.e. it is almost passive income. When your passive income exceeds your expenses, then you can be classed as financially free.

How does that sound? Become financially independent by having a passive income that exceeds all your expenses. Is this where you would like to be?

Methods of creating wealth

I didn't realize that there are three main ways to create wealth until I started to study this a few years ago. The three ways are:

- Start a business and, in this day and age, I suggest you should look at an internet business in the first instance
- The stock market
- Property

Rachel and I became financially free through property investment and more recently we have set up a couple of businesses. Our businesses are systemised and take very little of our time to manage. They are producing an income with hardly any input from us. These, like our houses, are generating income with only a little effort on our part.

Many wealthy people have either built their wealth through property or hold their wealth in property.

Lord Sugar bought £300m worth of property after he sold Amstrad, because he wanted somewhere safe to invest his money and to provide significant long term wealth. The properties are mostly trophy buildings around London, including Bond Street.

He felt that his electronics empire was the risky part of his business.

At a conference in 2011, he told the audience that he needs to learn more about property investment because the properties he bought have no mortgages. I think he realized that he should be leveraging the equity held in those properties.

Some examples of investing in assets that generate passive income

- **On-line products** - Create information products to be sold on-line

- **Business that (virtually) runs itself** - Create a business that can easily be systemised so you spend only a small amount of time 'on the business'

- **Network Marketing** – Tell a person about a product or service that you are passionate about. The product is one that is used on a regular basis so requires ongoing purchases, such as electricity. If the person buys the product, then you will receive commission on an ongoing basis all the time the person continues to buy. Do a job once and get paid over and over for it.

- **Income-generating assets** - Purchase or take control of an asset that generates income (e.g. property)

Top Tip Some of these ideas have very little start-up costs. You should aim to spend 5 to 10 hours per week on your chosen idea. This will bring you good returns for investing a little of your time.

Although I consider myself to be financially free, I still work a little ... because I enjoy it. To illustrate my current position, I would now like to quote T. Harv Eker, the motivational speaker, businessman and author of the book 'Secrets of the Millionaire Mind'.

· · · · ·

My part-time business is managing and investing my money and creating passive income streams

T. Harv Eker

· · · · ·

Probably the most important aspect to becoming wealthy is to understand how to manage money and assets. I discuss this in depth in Chapter 10.

I hope I have helped you to understand the importance of learning:

- Why and how to start thinking differently
- How to leverage other peoples' money, time and knowledge
- How working in collaboration will help you to succeed
- How to create additional income ideas so that you can build an investment pot
- The benefits of investing in cash-generating assets.

Let me now tell you about my preferred investment opportunity – UK property

CHAPTER 3

Why invest in the UK property market – what it can do for you

The UK is a great place to buy property as an investment for your future because:

- UK buy-to-let mortgages allow:
  - You to leverage the lender's money
  - Inflation to erode away your mortgage debt over time
  - Your mortgage debt to be paid by someone else
- House prices will increase over time due to:
  - Housing demand
  - Location desirability
  - UK's limited land availability

- You receive positive cash flow when you invest in the *right* investment property
- Property investing, when done correctly, will significantly contribute to your pension provision.
- Investing in property is generally less volatile than the stock market and provides excellent returns, so I view property as a better investment
- You have favourable tax regulations

NOW is also the *best* time to buy because:

- You cannot go back in time

and, as I write this book in 2013:

- House prices are close to the bottom of this price dip
- There are lots of opportunities to buy with a discount
- People are not getting much, if any, return on their 'normal' savings
- Good training programmes are available to show you how to invest safely

Many people have concerns about buying property; along the lines of:

- I lost money when I had to move because my house price had dropped in value
- I have heard about people losing money through property investing
- What if house prices go down further?
- What if interest rates go up?
- What if I cannot rent my investment property out?
- And more

I understand these concerns and that is why I developed robust systems to minimise risks and take account of "what if ..." scenarios. This is why it is essential for you to read this book so that you can avoid the pitfalls that some 'would-be' investors tumble into. I build in factors of safety into my analysis. I ensure I have cash in a buffer account that acts as my 'insurance' pot and contingency fund.

Also, buying investment property is totally different to buying your own home. When bought with the techniques I show you in this book, you should never have to sell your investment property. This means that the property price in the short to medium term does not affect you. Your positive cash flow will ensure that you are not out of pocket.

Let me go through some of the reasons for buying property in the UK in a little more detail.

UK buy-to-let mortgages

Leverage the Lender's Money

One of the reasons why UK property is such a good investment opportunity is because of the way buy-to-let mortgages operate. You can borrow money from someone else and make it work for your benefit. You do not need to pay back the borrowed money until sometime way into the future. You do not even need income from a salary to be able to borrow in this way, although you have more options if you do. I don't know of any other country that has these 'interest-only' buy-to-let mortgage options. All this is subject to each lender's specific criteria for lending.

Inflation erodes your mortgage debt over time

When you take out an 'interest only' mortgage to purchase your investment property, you only pay the interest on the amount borrowed. You do not pay off any of the mortgage loan. Due to inflation, this mortgage debt actually reduces over time. The buying power of £10,000 today is much less than it was twenty years ago. The mortgage loan value works along the same lines. If you borrow £100,000 today, in twenty years time you would not be able to buy so much with it; effectively inflation reduces your debt over time.

Your mortgage debt is being paid for by someone else

Using a mortgage loan, you are leveraging the bank's money. And the great thing about this is that you are not paying for the loan yourself. This is often referred to as "good debt" because your tenant is servicing your debt and your property running costs and even giving some profit in your pocket as well. In addition, you are obtaining the equity growth and you are getting some cash in as well – brilliant.

What is Equity?

Equity is the £ value that a person has in a business, property, or asset after paying off the outstanding loans and debts held against it.

If the likely selling price of your house was £150,000 and you have a £30,000 mortgage, then your equity would be £120,000.

UK house prices increase over the long term

Housing demand

There are more people needing homes in the UK than at any other time. The British population rose by 10 million between 1950 and 2000. The population in 2012 of 62 million is expected to continue to grow at a rate of 0.8% a year increasing by 4.9 million to 67.2 million by 2020 and 73 million by 2035 says the Office of National Statistics (ONS).

There has always been a shortfall in the number of houses built compared to the number of people that need a place to live. This has been compounded over the last couple of years when hardly any new homes have been built and the 'stock' of already built houses has virtually been cleared.

Even if the correct number of houses were being built using data from 5 years ago, there would still be a shortfall because more housing is needed to accommodate two further factors:

- The family home is changing. More and more people are choosing to live alone

- In addition, there is a net inflow of people coming into this country to live and work (net migration). Net migration increased to 198,000 in 2009 compared with 163,000 in the previous year. An estimated 572,000 people entered UK on a long term basis in the year to June 2010 while 346,000 emigrated (source ONS). This is an influx of over 225,000 people needing accommodation.

Location desirability (great capital growth strategy)

As well as natural inflation, property prices increase even more in the medium term due to desirability of certain locations, such as London and some other local regions. These are where people want to buy homes to live in, no matter what the economic circumstances of the country are.

Creating capital growth from location is similar but not the same as creating growth from inflation. We are looking for specific locations across the UK where the demand is based upon the continued desire of some people to live in that specific location.

Limited land on which to build

There is limited land in UK on which to build. There are only very few places in the world where this occurs; places such as Hong Kong and some other major cities. Because the land is needed, the price of land goes up and therefore any property built on that land becomes more valuable.

> The reason this book is about UK property is because I believe we have a stable and sustained need for property in the UK over the long term

Buying oversees property is not an investment

Buying property overseas is much more risky than buying in the UK and therefore is not a good investment. Some of the complexities and differences are language, law, mortgage products, exchange rates and taxes. Most people don't even know the relevant rules and regulations in this country, let alone overseas.

The vast majority of overseas property prices are led by new development prices. When new properties are built people tend to want the latest ones so they are willing to pay more for them. The older ones become less in demand and prices do not rise in line with the new build.

Most countries have ample land to build on: they are not limited by a scarce resource and can build on indefinitely. After a while, the destination as a whole becomes less attractive, or unaffordable and gradually there are more properties than people want. We have seen this in some parts of Spain in the last few years.

So, in general, unless careful and thorough research is undertaken, overseas property prices are more difficult to analyse and it is more difficult to predict what will happen over the long term

UK Property prices since 1952

You can see on the graphs that follow how property values increase over time; resulting in the creation of long term wealth for you as the trend continues. The source of the data I have used is http://www.nationwide.co.uk/hpi/datadownload/data_download.htm

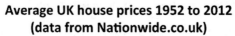

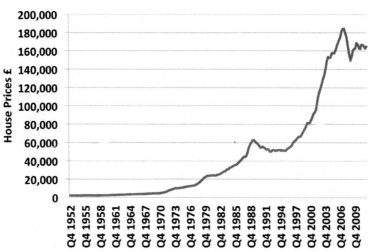

By looking at this graph, we learn that

- The average UK house price has increased by an average of 8.2% per annum over the entire period

- The average UK house price has increased since 1983 by an average of 16.7% per annum. This is equivalent to 6.3% year on year compounding growth.

- House prices double on average every 10 years

- There are periods of better growth and some periods where prices fall, but overall the trend is overwhelmingly upwards

- Property creates more long term wealth than most people could earn from a job

Receive positive cash flow from property

One of the fundamental rules you need to know about property investment is, to ensure that you always generate positive cash flow from the property. This always keeps your head above water, whether the price of property goes up or down. It's always making you money. It speeds up your timescale to financial freedom if you can use the cash generated to put into another investment property rather than spend it.

Property investing, when done correctly, will significantly contribute to your pension provision.

I have found that I no longer need to worry about my pension. My property income far exceeds the pension I am likely to get from the Government. So, I will not have to rely on them or anyone else to help me get through later life. I will not have to 'downsize' to sustain my way of life. My properties have become my pension.

Comparison between property and stock market investment

I hear discussions suggesting shares produce better returns than property. I will share with you my thoughts on this through several graphs.

Property values since 1983

I have used the same base data as before showing changes in property values as the previous graph, but I have added a line which represents the compounding growth in house prices of 6.6% year on year.

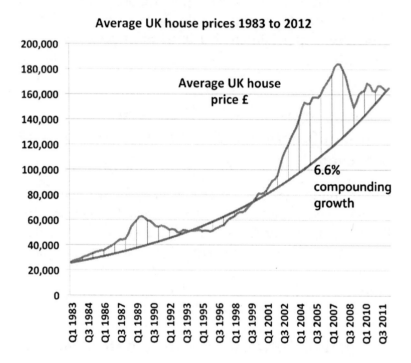

Average UK house prices 1983 to 2012

FTSE 100 share price index since 1983

I have used the FTSE 100 share price index data since 1983 as provided by www.finance.yahoo.com

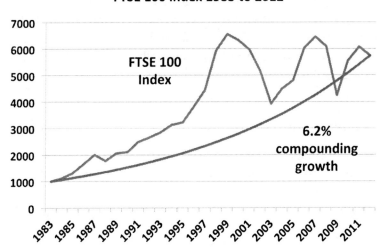

FTSE 100 index 1983 to 2012

Looking at this graph, we learn that

- The FTSE 100 index has increased since 1983 by an average of 16.3% per annum. This is equivalent to 6.2% year on year compounding growth.

- There are periods of better growth and some periods where prices fall.

- The overall trend is upwards but since 1999 the index has been moving sideways. As many investors do not sell their shares; the value of their investment has not increased over this 13 year period

Clearly these are average values and individual share prices will vary. Some will perform better and some will perform worse.

Conclusion

Since 1983, both the average UK property price and the FTSE 100 have increased by approximately 6% compounding growth year on year.

The graphs say to me that, in general, investing in property is less volatile than the stock market and it provides excellent returns. There is something else though, that makes investing in property especially attractive to me; the power of leverage.

Projecting into the future

For the purpose of analysis, we have £50,000 to invest in either shares or property. I will assume both investments will increase in value equivalent to 6% compounding growth per annum (similar to what my analysis of history has shown).

Invest £50,000 in shares

My first graph assumes that we have £50,000 and we decide to buy shares. Over 18 years our £50,000 would have a value of £135,000. This is an increase of 2.7 times our original investment; providing a **Return on Investment (ROI) for shares of 270%** over an 18 year period.

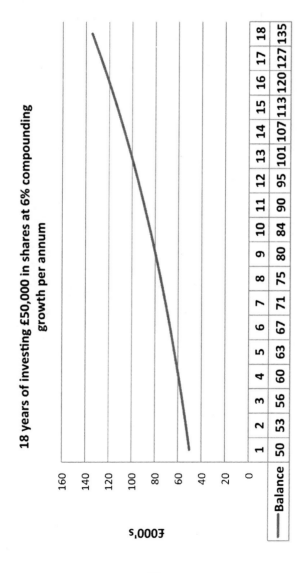

Balance	50	53	56	60	63	67	71	75	80	84	90	95	101	107	113	120	127	135
	1	2	3	4	5	6	7	8	9	10	11	12	13	14	15	16	17	18

18 years of investing £50,000 in shares at 6% compounding growth per annum

£000's

Invest £50,000 in property,

If we invest £50,000 into property, we can buy a house for £180,000 as set out below:

Our £50,000 will be used as follows:

- £5,000 for purchasing and setting up costs and
- £45,000 as a 25% deposit towards a property valued at £180,000. The £45,000 is your equity.
- The mortgage loan from the bank will be 75% of the property value = £135,000

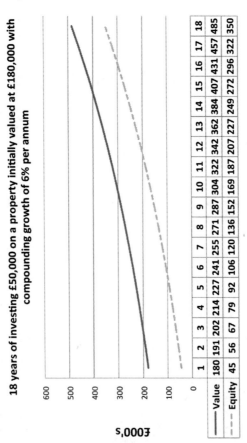

18 years of investing £50,000 on a property initially valued at £180,000 with compounding growth of 6% per annum

	1	2	3	4	5	6	7	8	9	10	11	12	13	14	15	16	17	18
Value	180	191	202	214	227	241	255	271	287	304	322	342	362	384	407	431	457	485
Equity	45	56	67	79	92	106	120	136	152	169	187	207	227	249	272	296	322	350

£000's

You can see that the house value appreciates at 6% and so is worth £485,000 after 18 years. The resulting equity is £485,000 less our mortgage of £135,000 which equals £350,000. This has grown from our initial £45,000.

In calculating our investment return we must take account of purchase costs so our initial investment of £50,000 returned us £350,000, providing an **ROI for property of 700%** over an 18 year period.

This is not the whole story though.

What if you want to use some of the growth for yourself in a few years time?

Retire Early Retire Wealthy - Your essential guide to Successful Property Investing

Take £20,000 out of your share investment

If you decide that you want to take out some money, maybe £20,000 for a wedding or similar, in year 5, then this graph shows that you end up with a final investment of £92,000, providing a **reduction in the return on investment to only 184%**. Taking money out has significantly affected the long term investment value.

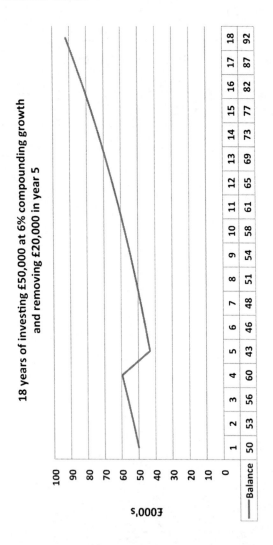

18 years of investing £50,000 at 6% compounding growth and removing £20,000 in year 5

£000's

	1	2	3	4	5	6	7	8	9	10	11	12	13	14	15	16	17	18
Balance	50	53	56	60	43	46	48	51	54	58	61	65	69	73	77	82	87	92

Take £20,000 out of your property investment

If you take £20,000 from your property, the end result is hardly affected because the property value doesn't change. The investment still continues to grow in value whether you have a large mortgage or none at all.

The way we take money out of the property is to remortgage. In our example, the mortgage would go up from £135,000 to £155,000. Your equity, after 18 years, would be £485,000 less your new mortgage of £155,000 and, is equal to £330,000; **still an impressive ROI of 660%.**

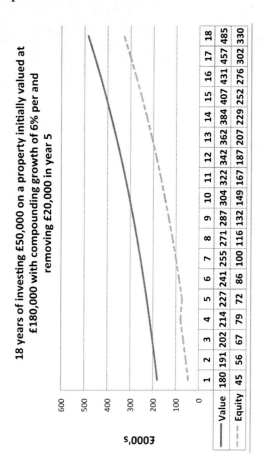

18 years of investing £50,000 on a property initially valued at £180,000 with compounding growth of 6% per and removing £20,000 in year 5

£000's

	1	2	3	4	5	6	7	8	9	10	11	12	13	14	15	16	17	18
Value	180	191	202	214	227	241	255	271	287	304	322	342	362	384	407	431	457	485
Equity	45	56	67	79	72	86	100	116	132	149	167	187	207	229	252	276	302	330

So, even if you ignore the £20,000 cash you now have in your pocket, this means the initial £50,000 is still worth £330,000, a gain of 660%. **WOW**!

It is for these reasons why I believe property is a better investment than shares.

Taxation and property

Top Tip When you take out equity from a property by remortgaging it, as in the scenario above, the cash extracted is totally tax free *provided* you reinvest it back into another property.

Even the cost of remortgaging the property is an allowable expense against any income tax you are due to pay from your property income. This tax rule is a massive benefit in creating wealth through property.

You will be charged income tax based upon the difference between your actual income from the rent and the allowable expenses.

Allowable expenses are those incurred running your investment property and I discuss these in more detail later. So the net income you receive from your investment property is taxed and the remainder is yours which can be saved or reinvested.

You will pay income tax annually. Your Accountant will be able to advise you specifically.

EXERCISE

Has your home increased in value?

The first time most people become aware of long term property growth is looking back at the values of their previous homes. If you have owned a house for more than 5 years, then your home is probably worth more than when you originally bought it.

Why not take a moment to consider ALL your home purchases and add in your parents' ones as well, especially if you have not bought one yourself yet.

Property	Bought for £k	Sold for £k	Difference £k	Number of year's owned
TOTAL				

Provided you have owned a property for more than 5 years, I would be very surprised if the difference between buying and selling your homes has not been a profitable one.

Now imagine if you had kept them all rather than sell them. What would they be worth now?

What if I can show you a way that you can do this from now on? Keep your home when you move and still be able to buy your new one; would that interest you? Yes – I'm helping you to *Retire Early Retire Wealthy*. Why not have a look at the website for the next workshop near you.

As I write this book, the UK and most of the world economies are in turmoil and properties are being bought and sold at prices far lower than people could have imagined a couple of years ago, so this is a particularly good time to start your property portfolio.

No one can know if we have reached the absolute bottom of the recession, but one thing is for sure, we are very close to it.

As my strategy is to build a portfolio for long term growth, now is an excellent time to start buying UK property.

PART II

Knowing the fundamentals can make your dreams a reality

Many people get on the property bandwagon with the notion that buying a property is all you have to do to be an investor, believing that it is easy. However, I have seen many property portfolios which do not work.

Investing in property can be complex which is why I teach the fundamentals of property investment first. These are the basic building blocks for everything else. Learning the fundamentals will give you a firm foundation from which you can build up your property investment safely. You will be able to do the analysis without even leaving your armchair.

A fundamental mistake, for example, is buying in a

development where most of the properties are bought by other investors; even though you may have been offered the property at a 'bargain' price. The reason is that there is too much competition. When you want to rent out your property you have to keep your rent low to attract a tenant otherwise they will go elsewhere. When you want to sell the property, the price you can ask for it will be a reflection of the person wanting to buy it. With a development made up of tenanted property, there is a limited potential buying market, so prices will not rise as fast as other locations. It might be difficult to sell. There are only a very few exceptions to this rule.

There are many other mistakes some investors make. But understanding and applying the fundamentals, to purchasing property, is likely to save you a lot of heartache. My aim is to teach the basics of how property can help you to *create wealth – so that the rest of your life can follow.*

Top Tip Become a professional; this is a business, not a hobby.

When you invest professionally, you should receive money in your pocket each month providing positive cash flow and over the long term you will increase your wealth. Do not be tempted to buy a property that does not comply with these fundamentals because it is unlikely to work without a struggle for many years.

In this part of the book, you will learn several ways to generate 'long term wealth' and 'income' from property; the principles of investing in UK property; how to think about property in an objective way: what to consider; where to buy; what to buy and what price to pay. I will show you how to *buy the right property in the right location at the right price*. The fundamentals!

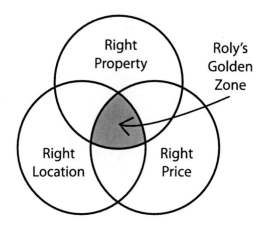

Right Property

Roly's Golden Zone

Right Location

Right Price

ROLY'S GOLDEN ZONE –

Buying the right property in the right location at the right price

CHAPTER 4

Investing in property - helping you create your life

In order to create the life you desire you need to create long term wealth. To ensure your dream does not go sour you must have enough cash coming in to cover your investment costs. When done properly, investing in UK property is secure and creates both:

- long term wealth and
- positive cash flow

Four ways to generate 'long term wealth' from property

There are four basic ways that wealth can be generated when you invest in property. These four ways work both independently and together, depending upon the economic conditions. Also it is worth noting that some of the strategies work all the time; but others are more susceptible to economic conditions.

The four ways to generate long term wealth from property are:

- Capital growth from inflation
- Capital growth from location desirability
- Adding value (e.g. "doing it up" and adding a bedroom)
- Buy property at a discount

Capital growth from inflation

Property inflation is driven by a general demand for property but there are times, like 2009 to 2012, when this type of growth does not occur. The housing market prices are correcting themselves to align with other national and global economic needs.

Top Tip Creating capital growth from inflation is something I do NOT want to rely on too much to build your portfolio, especially during a depressed housing market.

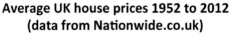

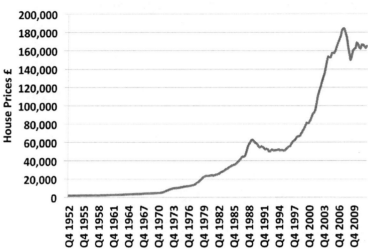

You can see however, that property values do increase over time and this will result in creating long term wealth for you.

Capital growth from a desirable location

Wealth is also created from property in the medium term due to desirable location. In areas, such as London and some other local regions, people want to buy homes to live in, no matter what the economic circumstances of the country are. We are looking for specific locations across the UK where the demand is based upon the continued desire of some people to live in that specific location.

Take a look at the graph of property prices by region. London and the South of England have fared much better than other parts of UK when looking at average house prices.

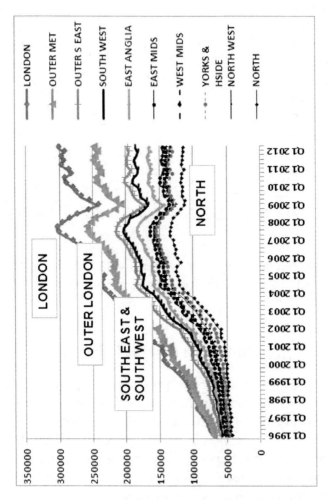

Looking at the graph, we see that the 1996 average regional property values were between £43k and £71k. By the end of 2011, London had increased to around £300k (421%).

The North had increased to £116k (267%).

If we assess the London data in more detail:

- A property valued at £71,000 in 1996 could have a 75% loan to value buy-to-let mortgage of £53,250 giving us equity of £17,750.

- If we did not remortgage that property, then the equity would now be £300,000 - £53,250 = £246,750.

- This gives an increase in equity from £17,750 to £246,750 = £229,000 using only £17,750 of your own money.

- This is an average rise of over £15k per year: equivalent to 86% per annum Return on Investment. WOW!

This also demonstrates that the original mortgage debt effectively reduces over time.

This gives us a clue where to buy if we want to create long term wealth, although there will be pockets within the 'lower' increased regions where growth would be high. We just need to delve down into the numbers some more.

At a local level, we can also look at the local community demographic make-up at various locations across the UK. From this we can anticipate the community needs. The councils do this all the time and they produce plans that are available for us to use. We are specifically looking to fulfil a community need: in our case, housing. We then look at the current housing situation. If there appears to be insufficient houses for the current or predicted demand, then this might be a good place to start buying. House prices will go up, regardless of the national economic condition.

In these cases we are not relying on general countrywide inflation, just specific locations where, say, there are increasing jobs or a particular and valued way of life.

To complete the picture, we can look at the data of property prices by UK country.

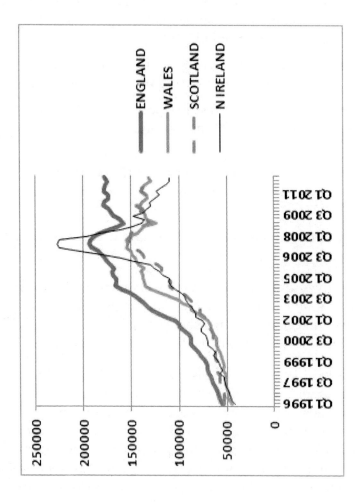

England has had a higher growth rate than the other UK countries overall. N Ireland had a boom few years but the negative correction has been just as big. This data illustrates that you must carry out good analysis. My system, which I call Roly's Property Analyser that I discuss later, told me in March 2006 that "the numbers do not work". The fundamentals showed me that buying a property in the location I was interested in, would not work. The result was that I stopped buying property for a few years until the numbers worked again.

Adding value

There are several ways to add value to your investment property.

Worst House + *Do some work* = *Best House*

One strategy is to buy a property at a low value; do some specific work to make it attractive; and by doing so you increase its value to be similar to, or better than, the best house on the street! You have now increased your equity in the property.

Another way is by adding rooms to your property. Many people believe this can be achieved by adding an extension, putting on a conservatory and creating an extra room, for example. This does add some value, but the investor's choice is, only create extra bedrooms.

I explain both of these strategies in more detail later in Chapter 5.

Buy property at a discount

Once you become knowledgeable about how to 'make the numbers work', you will appreciate that it is highly desirable to create the maximum equity in your investment property from day one. One way to do this - is to buy the property at a price below the price that regular homeowners buy it for. I tell you more about how to do this in a later chapter. We are generally looking for a reduction of at least a 15% on the value which a surveyor, from the Registered Institution of Chartered Surveyors (RICS), would give the property.

As soon as you have made the purchase with a discount, you are effectively 'in the money'. You are probably going to have to give the property a good clean up and maybe some light refurbishment. The value of your property should now be worth more than the price you paid for it, even allowing for all your expenses.

Three ways to generate 'income' from property

You can generate income by renting out your property for more than the amount you are paying, both to borrow the money needed to buy it and to cover the running costs. This is generally called cash-flow because you receive money every month. This is used to support all of your investments. There are two ways associated with this that I call

- 'High cash flow' and
- 'Combo' (cash flow and capital growth)

There is a third strategy:

- Buying a property and selling it on.

Each strategy has advantages and disadvantages.

The amount of income generated from these methods will vary depending upon the strategy you choose.

High cash flow – Houses in Multiple Occupation (HMOs)

Properties that provide high cash flow are generally associated with larger dwellings that are rented out on a room by room basis, generally 4 or more rooms. These are called Houses in Multiple Occupation or HMOs for short. The idea here is that you get a better return on your money because you receive higher income from several people sharing, than from a single family in a big house.

Typically 5 single people could share a good size 5 bed family house. The rent from a family could be around £1200 per month whereas the 5 sharers might pay around £400 each. This would give you an income of £2000 per month. You do have more expenses and higher running costs but you still end up with a better cash flow than with a family, if done correctly.

House in Multiple Occupation (HMO) is a defined term in law and as such you will have to abide by the strict laws that govern this type of dwelling.

There are some general significant advantages and disadvantages of HMOs over single let properties:

Advantages

- Higher monthly income resulting from the same capital outlay
- Proportionally less void periods

What is a void period?

When your property is not rented out, you have a period where you receive no rent. This is called a void period. For an HMO, if one room is not rented, then you only lose rent for one room and not the whole house.

Disadvantages

- Higher capital investment because you are buying larger properties
- Smaller loan to value borrowing ratio so you will need to put in a deposit of at least 35% of the value of the property
- Need to fully furnish the property
- Higher maintenance and running costs (including utility bills)
- Need to address the tenant's personality traits
- Several individual tenancy agreements in the same property

High cash flow – family demand locations

A second high cash flow type of property can be found in some locations in the UK and is a traditional buy-to let property. The idea here is that you can buy the property relatively cheaply compared with other similar properties but the demand for rental is high, resulting in a very good cash flow.

Advantages

- Higher monthly income than the average
- You do not have to put so much of your own money into the purchase as HMOs.

Disadvantages

- Due to the locality of these types of property, you may not get as much capital growth as you would expect in other regions / locations of the country.

'Combo' (cash flow and capital growth)

Buying a traditional home that will be rented out to one person or family to provide positive cash flow is a sound proposition when you are in a 'good growth' location.

Advantages

- You will not need to put so much of your own money in as an HMO.
- Good capital growth

Disadvantages

- Cash flow during high mortgage interest rate periods may be small

Buy and sell

The strategy of buy and sell has been a favourite strategy of many builders throughout time. This involves buying a property, 'doing it up' and then selling it at a profit. This could involve refurbishing an old house; maybe carrying out some structural work; or even knocking an old place down and building something new.

The idea is not to hold onto the property for very long.

Although I am showing you how to create long term wealth, there are times when generating some extra cash this way can be useful.

This strategy is not so easily implemented during a depressed housing market because there are fewer buyers around and selling it may prove difficult and time consuming.

You MUST have an alternative exit strategy. You may say "if I cannot sell the property for the price I want, then I will rent it out". You will need to check that 'the numbers work' as a rental property as well as a 'buy and sell' one.

How investing in property works in practice, when you do it correctly

Example

I am investigating whether this 2 bed house is worth buying. The house is on the market for £114,000 but it needs some work doing to it. If I spend £2000, it will be at least as good as the other houses on the street that are on the market for £123,000. In its improved condition I will be able to rent it out at £600 per month.

The seller needs to sell quickly to take up a new job elsewhere, so I believe I can purchase this house at £96,000. My due diligence (homework) tells me that there is good demand for these types of houses, so I will allow for a 9% growth within a year or so.

The strategy I am going to use is:

- Buy the property with a discount
- Add value because it is an older property in need of a little attention
- Buy in a desirable location and rent it out to our target market
- Ensure incoming rent exceeds all running costs
- Refinance the property at the right time
- Use proceeds to purchase another

INITIAL COSTS - Buying the Property		
Buy the property - price		£96,000
Legal costs		£2,000
Add Value (do work)		£2,000
TOTAL COSTS		**£100,000**
I am going to FUND this by:		
Buy-to-let mortgage at 75% loan to property value (purchase price x 75%)		
75% Mortgage	£72,000	
The remainder of the money needed will come from my own funds	£28,000	
TOTAL USED		£100,000
Having done some work, the property is now worth £123,000		

MONTHLY CASH FLOW		
ONGOING EXPENSES		
Cost of the mortgage, for this example, will be 5% per annum. Monthly cost of mortgage will therefore be 5% x £72,000 divided by 12 months = £300 per month		
I will pay a Letting Agent to manage the property and tenants, and also make an allowance for other items. I discuss these in more detail in Chapter 8.		
Mortgage		£300
Letting Agent Fees		£60
Maintenance		£30
Contingency		£20
TOTAL EXPENSES		**£410**
FUNDED BY - The rent from the tenant each month		
Rent from tenant	**£600**	
POSITIVE CASH FLOW		**£190**
This property generates more income than expenses		

Top Tip Create a BUFFER

Do not invest ALL your initial cash. Some of it, around 5% to 10%, should be put into your bank account AND NOT used, except for emergency situations with regard to your property portfolio.

This is a safety net; an insurance protection against expenses such as high interest rises and unknowns, such as the need to replace a boiler. I discuss this more in Chapter 8 Step 1.

Refinance the property

At some time in the future, with a target time of 12 to 15 months, ask a new Lender to revalue the property which will have risen in value.

In this scenario, we bought:

- at a discount and
- we added value

This raised the value of the property to the same as other good quality houses in the street, £123,000.

REFINANCING		
Once we had done the work when we first bought the property, its value rose to		£123,000
We also bought in a high demand location generally rising around 9% per annum, so in 14 months the value rose by: £13,000		
New Property Value		**£136,000**
So now, we take out a new mortgage		
New 75% Mortgage	**£102,000**	
THIS PAYS BACK OUR ORIGINAL OUTLAY		
Original Mortgage	£72,000	
Money to start again	**£30,000**	
This is more than the original £28,000 of our own money that we put into the property in the beginning. **That's what we like!**		

Does the property still generate monthly cash flow?

Top Tip Check that you still receive a monthly positive cash flow after refinancing

The new monthly cost of the mortgage will now be 5% x £102,000 divided by 12 months = £425 per month.

NEW MONTHLY CASH FLOW		
ONGOING EXPENSES		
Mortgage		£425
Letting Agent Fees		£60
Maintenance		£30
Contingency		£20
TOTAL EXPENSES		£535
FUNDED BY		
The rent increases from £600 by		
around 3% (say) to £620 per month	**£620**	
POSITIVE CASH FLOW		**£85**
The result of this ideal scenario is that we obtain a monthly cash positive property that has none of our own money left in.		

This is how creating wealth works.

Infinite return on cash employed

Rachel and I have now progressed to have *infinite return on most of our investment properties* because we have refinanced and taken out all of our original money. We have no money left in! This means that all the cash we receive now is generated from 'nothing'! WOW!

This is the secret that investing in property uncovers. The increase in the value of the property has generated wealth that, in turn, allows you to refinance and then starts to generate money without your input. This has leveraged other people's money (the bank's, in this case).

In summary:

- Buy a property using some of your own money and some money from a lender, normally a bank or building society. The lender's money will be in the form of a buy-to-let mortgage.

- Buy the right property in the right location at the right price (Chapter 5)

- Add value to the property by doing a little work to it

- Rent the property out to a tenant who will pay you a monthly rent

- The rental income will exceed the expenses and so generates a net monthly income

- Open an 'investment property bank account' which your income and outgoings will be managed from

- Open a 'buffer bank account' which will only be used to pay for large, unexpected property related items. Replenish this from your 'investment property account' when appropriate.

- Do not spend any accrued profit, because you want to re-invest this in order to create your long term wealth

- Refinance the property when the time is right and re-invest the income into another property

Now, you can begin to see how you can become wealthy through property investment.

You are protected from financial risk because (i) you have a buffer which can be used to offset interest rate rises and (ii) you buy property at *the right property in the right location at the right price,* which I discuss in Chapter 5. This protects you from property values falling below your purchase price – should you ever need to sell.

Rachel and I do not intend to sell, for a long time anyway: and therefore we do not have to worry if property prices fall, because we will not realize any financial loss.

Many investors may not believe me, because they have not got this far yet. I have found this is mainly because they have not bought the correct house in the beginning or they have passively acquired it.

The most profitable way this works is when you buy the right property in the right location at the right price.

CHAPTER 5

Buying the right property in the right location at the right price

By now, you may have realized there are many property investment opportunities. The essential ingredient for ensuring that the strategies I mention in this book work in practice comes down to *buying the right property in the right location at the right price*.

As you might imagine, this is complex. I look upon this as my property jigsaw puzzle and this is definitely one very large puzzle!

Rachel and I have proven systems that give you the greatest chance of success. Our system relies on **knowing** the numbers that ensure that we *buy the right property in the right location at the right price.*

Tenant type

It is important to know who your target market is when you start to think about investing. Each type of renter will have a different need. For example, most young single renters will want to be close to town or university. A young family on the other hand, would want a good school or social community close by.

A few tenant types are:

- Families
- Single
- Sharing friends
- Sharing within an HMO
- Young professional
- Students
- Non-professional
- People on benefits
- People on short-term overseas contracts
- People on short and medium term job-relocation

The priority of a tenant is generally: number of bedrooms / property type / price per month / location and then any add-ons such as garage and great condition. So if the best value property to buy is not in very good condition – that's ok – we can fix that easily – to the standard expected by our target tenant.

It is worth noting:

- That many young professionals who want to house share, require their shared accommodation to be of a high standard

- The average age of the 1st time buyer is 38 years old (as reported by moneysupermarket.com in May 2011).

Roly's Golden Zone – the ONLY place to buy

Roly's Golden Zone is where the three attributes of right property type, right location and right price combine. You cannot separate these attributes; the right property *must* be in the right location and you *must* only buy it if it is at the right price. If any of these do not correspond to each other, then it will not work. You could be offered a great looking property for a really good price but if it is in a location that nobody wants to rent in, then it will not work. All these three elements are interlinked.

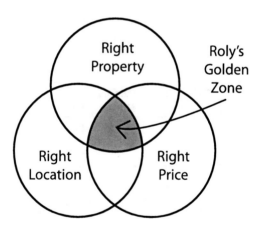

I believe this is where many investors struggle. They often buy a property close to where they live – and this is fine – but if the location is a village or a small town, then there may not be a high demand for rented property. This results in difficulty achieving adequate rent to cover all costs and there are likely to be long periods when the property is vacant without any rent at all.

A professional property investor will decide whether to buy or not, based upon calculated numbers. If the numbers work, it will enter the consideration phase. If it does not, it will be discarded. The non-professional becomes attached to a property because it is cheap or well decorated or has a lovely garden. This is not the way to buy an investment property.

You are therefore looking to identify the property that will cost you the least to 'get it tenanted'. This means the cost will be a combination of: purchase price; purchase costs; cost of any work to get the property to the appropriate standard to rent it out; and the cost of finding a tenant.

Buying the right property

There are several strategies that can be employed to *buy the right property*. The strategies can be combined to suit the opportunity.

Strategy	Older flat	Older House	HMO	New property
Buy the worst house on best street	Yes	Yes	Yes	
Do it up to add value	Yes	Yes	Yes	
Add additional bedrooms **		Ideally	Unlikely	
Split rentals of larger houses **		Maybe	Unlikely	Maybe
Change use to HMO **		Maybe	Done	Maybe
Buy with a discount price ***	Yes	Yes	Yes	Yes

** Alterations to property may need Local Authority approval. You will need to investigate this BEFORE making the purchase if you are relying upon this to make the investment work for you. Sub-dividing properties and converting to HMOs is a topic too large to cover in this book. If you want to know more, then please let me know through the contact page of my website, www.mylifesolutions.co.uk

*** Buying with a discount is discussed a little later in "Buying the property at the right price" section.

Worst house on the best street

 Buying the worst house on the best street is the most basic criterion to a professional investor, but is often not considered by many people, even some investors!

The worst house implies that some work will be required to the property we are looking for. Most people, looking for a house to live in, would probably walk on by. The house would be unkempt and in need of love and care. Investors like these properties, because making it looking great again is a fairly easy job. The idea is that we pick up a bargain because nobody else wants it.

My statement also says 'best street'. People will always want to live on the best street if they can afford it because it is a desirable location. This means this street will always be in demand.

Before you start your property analysis, decide upon your preferred tenant type because this dictates the type of property you should be looking for. Alternatively, you could have a couple of possibilities and do the analysis on both. For my example below, I am looking for a two-bed property suitable for two 'sharers' or a young couple, who may or may not have a child.

The analysis process is as follows:

1. Look at all the property sales details of all the 2 bed houses for sale in the same street or locality.

2. The idea is to compare like for like properties.

3. Identify the differences between the various properties such as condition/garage/heating/double glazing

4. You will now have a range of prices and conditions

5. You will need to estimate the cost of any work required to bring the property up to standard

6. You should then be able to decide which ones will be the best to consider

7. Clearly if you can get a clean and tidy house with no work for the cheapest price, then this would be the one on the street to consider buying.

8. Remember though, you will not be living in it yourself. The majority of tenants won't mind too much. Their priority generally is property type / number of bedrooms / price per month / location and then any add-ons such as garage and great condition. So if the best value property to buy is not in very good condition – that's ok – we can fix that easily.

9. Repeat this for any other property types you are interested in on the street or in the locality.

The conclusion of this analysis will be to identify several properties that might be worth looking at in more detail. You are now in a position to start collecting specific information that will be used in our data analysis. I use Roly's Property Analyser, which I tell you about in Chapter 7.

From experience, the cheapest ones on the market often need some work doing to them to bring them up to letting standard.

We can now take a look at how to add value to a property to make it worth more.

Do it up to add value

There are several ways to add value to a property to make it worth more.

A good clean up

 The quickest and cheapest way to add immediate value is to buy a property that has been neglected a little. The smellier the better, as most home buyers will be put off.

Sometimes the property only needs a good clean: the kitchen including the cooker, hob and extractor fans; the bathroom; floors etc. Some of the flooring may need replacing and some paintwork might need refreshing.

You will probably need to do some gardening. This is especially important at the front of the house where people drive by 'to take an initial look'. You want them to be so impressed that they want to come and look inside. You will need to do some cleaning of the windows and window frames and maybe a little painting. This is called 'kerb appeal'.

This could add a few thousand pounds of value because a

regular home owner can now walk into the property and live in it without having to do anything much.

There are cleaning firms and handymen that do all these jobs, either as a job-lot or as individual items of work. For example, you could use a local specialist cooker cleaning company and a local gardener rather than a single handyman. The professional cooker cleaner will cost around £70 and would make the cooker look like new in a couple of hours.

Light refurbishment

I suggest that a light refurbishment is where any general handy person could do the work themselves. This would also include putting in a new kitchen and bathroom where a tradesman could be employed and will give you a fixed price. You could consider employing a 'bath doctor' to refurbish the bath etc.

A light refurbishment is when a property requires a little work to bring it up to a standard that is required by a residential buyer. This may involve redecoration, updating a bathroom and kitchen and tidying up the outside. Maybe you can replace the windows, but not much more.

Clear everything out; rubbish, carpets, curtains, wall fixings, everything. Then give it a thorough clean up and scrub down, filling any holes in walls etc. You will need to do some painting of the walls, skirting boards and ceilings to freshen it up. You may also need to tighten door and window locks, taps, etc. You should either clean the cooker or replace it. Then replace the flooring.

The cost of a good clean and a refreshment of the paintwork is not expensive. A new kitchen might be around £3000 and bathroom, £1500.

Top Tip If the cost of any 'refurbishment' work does not add at least 2 times the cost of the work, to the value of the property – don't do it – it will generally not be cost/time effective.

This work should be finished within 1, maybe 2 weeks absolute maximum.

The strategy is to buy a property at a low value, do some specific work to make it attractive and increase its value to be similar or better than the best house on the street! You have now increased your equity in the property.

Worst House   +   *Do some work*   =   *Best House*

Here is an example – our 4th property.

---

2 bed property, Blackbrook, Taunton – Light refurbishment

Rachel had become so confident after we had bought our first 3 properties that she went to look at this house without me even knowing!

The locality is very sought-after because it is a pleasant suburban area, within walking distance of a business park, 2 miles to town and only 2 miles to the motorway junction. Before Rachel went to look at this modern 2 bed terraced house, she did her homework. This area had a buoyant rental market and a 2 bed would rent for £485 per month. This was in a good locality as it was always in demand.

The property was on market for £109,000 and needed some love and care and, in Rachel's considered view, all the windows needed replacing which would cost around £3,000.

Other houses in a better condition on the street were for sale for around £118,000. So, spending £3,000 would add around £9,000 which meets one of our criteria.

The estate agent knew us because we had bought from them before without any hitches. We had money available and a mortgage had been approved in principle. We could buy the property as quickly as the seller's solicitor could process the paperwork.

Even before telling me that she was viewing property, Rachel decided to make an offer of £102,000. The estate agent explained our circumstances to the seller and they finally agreed to sell to us at £104,000. So we had built in additional equity from day one.

Eleven months later in July 2004, the house was valued at £135,000 and so we took out a new mortgage of £105,000. This paid off the original mortgage and paid us back our deposit. We used this cash to finance another purchase.

Within our refinance calculations, we ensure that the rent covers our new costs.

We now had positive cash-flow which was being generated using very little of own money left in the property.

Now that's what we like!

Structural work

If the property needs structural work, like a new roof, just think again. Once you start messing around with walls and floorboards, then you are into the 'unknown' and the risks become higher. You will not be able to cost the potential work or the time needed so easily. Maybe everything will be ok and turn out as 'hoped' but just beware.

Structural work may include taking the walls back to the brickwork, changing the layout of the rooms, replacing windows and repairing the roof. You are likely to require several tradesmen working at the same time and it will typically take around 3 to 6 months.

This sort of project has lots of unknowns in terms of absolute costs and time scales therefore your cost analysis and budget will need to allow for this.

In this case not many residential buyers want to undertake this sort of work so the house price you pay will reflect this. In fact, not many investors take this sort of work on either; the perceived risks are too high for them.

Add bedrooms

Refurbishment of property is just one way to add value. There are other ways, for example, adding or creating another bedroom. This work can be done at any time – to suit your need and your wallet; either at the outset or sometime in the future.

The vast majority of the UK residential property is described in terms of number of bedrooms. If a property has more bedrooms than a similar property type in the same locality, then it will be valued higher than one with fewer bedrooms.

When you are looking at properties in a particular location, you should look to see what other people have done to their homes.

Some examples to look for:

- put a room in roof
- divided a very large bedroom into two
- moved an internal wall to create that extra bedroom
- converted a garage to a bedroom
- put an extension over the garage

Top Tip – Only add bedrooms

Adding or creating other types of living space such as conservatories do not generally add value. It might help to sell the property – to sell your house rather than a neighbour's, but you will not get 'that much' more. So for us, as professional investors, this is something we do not do often. Stick to adding bedrooms as a general rule.

Remember that it will generally not be cost/time effective adding another bedroom if the cost is £10,000 and it does not add at least £20,000 to the overall value of the property.

Buying the property at the right price

All the strategies for *buying the right property* will only work if you can buy the *property at the right price*.

The right purchase price is when the combination of actual purchase price; legal and other purchase costs and the cost of any works - is much less than the majority of the prices of similar properties. In a year's time after the property has been 'done-up', the aim is to convince a surveyor that it is worth the same as the best house on the street. The result we are looking for is to be able to refinance the property and take all, or most, of our own money back out.

So a common method used by professional investors is to buy property below Registered Institution of Chartered Surveyors' (RICS) valuation at the outset. Buying property with a discount ensures that you have additional equity in your property from day one. This safeguards you, even if prices go a 'little further down', in periods of property price uncertainty. The extra equity effectively becomes a buffer.

We are generally looking for at least 15% below RICS valuation and sometimes this can be as much as 40% (but rare). Big discounts are not achievable in all locations due to buyer demand, but what I am implying is that the discount must be more than just a few thousand pounds.

> **Top Tip** The bulk of the profit on property is made at the time of purchase; very little is gained at the time of disposal, so the property investment must work at the outset.

There are two ways to buy below RICS valuation that I would like to share with you at this time.

- Buying in bulk
- Buying from sellers that have time pressures

Buying in bulk

Firstly, let me say that my strategy for buying in bulk is through 'a little but often' approach, rather than all at the same time, or all in the same location. If we buy a whole or significant part of a development, which some property companies do, then this causes us, the professional investor, a problem. The property company gets the properties at a discount and that is fine, but they then sell them on to investors who will want to rent them out. The competition to find tenants becomes too much, resulting in lower rental charges; higher void periods and subdued selling prices.

By buying property 'a little but often', we can still get the discounts because the vendors know: we will keep coming back for more; we carry through on our promises to buy (so no wasted time and effort on their part) and we know the process so that we can complete quickly (often within 28 days).

The vendors I am talking about here are developers, estate agents (on behalf of the owners) and banks (who have already repossessed property that they do not want).

Buying from sellers who have time pressures

There are many reasons why some people need to sell their property quickly; job relocation, family bereavement and financial difficulty, to name a few.

Their prime aim is to move out as soon as possible. The sale price is less important than speed. If they are relocating, then they will pick up a bargain at the other end.

The vendor will be pleased to 'finally get an offer for their property' and from someone that has funds in place and who will exchange within a short timeframe.

There are many ways to find people who want to sell their house quickly, for example: attending auctions, leaflet dropping and on-line campaigns. This topic is so vast that it is a whole book in itself and finding these sorts of sellers often becomes a significant job. In the early days of your property investment journey, I suggest that you leave this element to full time professionals.

Other factors to consider

There are several other factors which affect the value of property. If you buy a property without considering these factors, you are likely to lose money. The sorts of things to be careful of are:

- Property that cannot be mortgaged
- Leasehold property with less than 85 years remaining on the lease
- Unusually constructed property

If you do your homework correctly though, you will identify these factors and can use it to your advantage. There are techniques for turning these properties into good options.

Analysis

By following the process of *buying the right property*, you will have arrived at a range of potential properties. Now knowing that you can buy at a discount, you can add this into the equation, i.e. you can now start thinking along the lines of "If I could buy house x for £x, then this would be the best deal". You can do this for all your potential purchases using Roly's Property Analyser that I describe in Chapter 7.

Choosing the right location

Finding *the right property at the right price* is not enough. It does not become the right property unless it is in the right location.

It is no good buying a property intending to let it out if there is no demand for rental property in that location. Even if it is cheap!

Top Tip Check out the rental potential

Talk to the letting agents in the area you are thinking about buying in. Ask them questions like:

"I have heard that town x is good for property investment. Are there any particular areas which rent out well?"

Follow this up with "why?" and "are there better towns?" or "are there specific areas?" and "what would that rent for?"

"Which areas do not rent well? ..."Why?" etc.

And if you have a locality in mind,

"I have seen a 2-bed house in x street, would that be any good? OR "is there a better street where people like to live? Why?"

The letting agent will be only too pleased to help, especially if you ask for one of their Letting Packs, implying you will be asking them to manage the tenancy for you.

So, hand in hand with looking for that bargain property, make sure it is in the right location. Choosing the right location is vitally important. It is probably *THE* most important aspect of good investment.

There are many reasons why people chose to live in one place rather than another such as:

- Good transport links
- Commuter belt for large cities

- Seaside location
- New employment opportunities
- Good schools
- University towns

And of course, there is no one right area. There are many areas that are good locations. The trick is to match your specific property investment strategy with the right location for that strategy. Over time, good locations change and become less sought after. Conversely, other locations become better.

Where you live

If your property strategy includes looking after your investment properties yourself, then you should buy properties within reasonable driving distance of where you live. In our experience we have found that if it is nearby, perhaps within 30 minutes, then we would go and inspect the property ourselves and investigate any faults. If it further away, then we ask a tradesmen to visit to find out why, say, the extractor fan has stopped working, instead of checking it out ourselves.

Here are some of the advantages and disadvantages of buying property close to where you live.

Advantages:

- You can check out problems yourself and only call tradesmen if you cannot do the job yourself - or don't want to. This is a cost saving to you (but maybe not the best use of your time)
- You know your area and you know the locations where xx types of people want to live and where yy

do not want to live. Based upon your target market you will know the specific areas to look in. There might be several areas in your town which might be suitable.

- You can keep in touch with your local estate agents and letting agents.

- You will know how property prices change from location to location

Disadvantages

- You may not obtain the highest growth on property prices

- You may not have sufficient capital to purchase in your area

- You may not obtain good cash flow

- The demand for rental properties may not be adequate to protect you from periods of voids (no tenants)

- You will be on call every day and night if you manage them yourself

In summary, buying locally is easier to manage and keep your finger on the pulse, but it may not be the best financial decision or best use of your time. Be certain to evaluate the financial decision fully.

Great cash flow locations

There are some areas in the UK where property provides very good cash flow. These are generally where there is a high tenant population and demand for rental property is high. If these locations are outside your immediate area, there are companies that offer to find properties in these areas. In most cases they even organise the work required to bring the property up to the rental standard. These are generally called sourcing companies. I do have a word of caution though: only use companies you know and trust and do not believe everything they say. Check any property they offer against the fundamentals I describe in this book. Check out the company thoroughly as well.

Advantages:

- Someone else will look after these properties and tenants for you, so you will not have to be on call every day and night

- Demand for rental properties are high and so void periods will be lower than many other areas

- The monthly rents are high in comparison to your purchase price and will therefore be sufficient to cover your expenses even with high interest rates

- A professional (sourcing company) will be finding the properties for you

- The professional will negotiate with the seller to get the best buying price for you – and this is likely to be significantly better than you could get yourself.

- You are not confined to the property stock in your locality – so the amount of money to purchase property may go further

Disadvantages:

- You will need to pay for someone to manage the properties for you - but this is included in the cost calculations to ensure the property still provides positive cash flow

- You will not be able to visit the property as often as you might think you should – but this turns out to be a good thing really – out of sight, out of mind!

- You will pay a small fee to the professional for their services – but this is offset within the discounted buying price

- The property may not rise in value in percentage terms as well as other locations in the UK

This is an excellent strategy if you want the great annual returns and some price growth

High growth areas

Earlier I showed you a graph of property growth by UK region. You may recall that London and Outer London were very high growth regions. However, there are parts of London that are better than most, and likewise there are some parts that are not so desirable. The same is true of pockets in other regions. So even in regions which have an average low or medium growth, there will be some high and some very low growth areas. My message is do not dismiss some parts of the country because of the region graphs I have shown you. Delve deeper into the numbers.

If these are outside your local area, then you can use sourcing companies to help you.

Summary - some attributes of Roly's Golden Zone

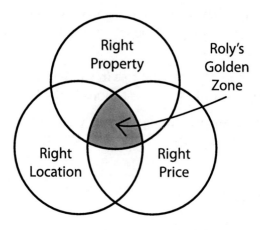

From my years of experience I can share with you some of the attributes of Roly's Golden Zone. These are a few specific rules that make the perfect purchase:

1. The rental income must be greater than all costs, now and in the future

2. There must be an underlying demand for rental property in this location

3. You do not want to compete with too many similar properties

4. If you are going to find the property yourself and manage it yourself, it must be within 30 to 45 minutes of your home

5. The property is likely to be one of the worst homes on the street rather than the best

6. Alternatively (to 5 above), it must be in a location of continued high demand, such as some specific parts of London

7. It would be advantageous if the property had scope for further development

8. Using the techniques I have described, there must be a reasonable chance of refinancing within 12 months to take out all or most of your original deposit.

9. Medium or long term maintenance must be minimal - unless the price reflects the potential costs - so that you can either (i) buy it for much less and use some of this 'discount' to put into your buffer account; or (ii) the cash flow is so good that it allows you to build up your buffer quickly.

10. Leasehold property must have at least 85 years remaining - unless the price reflects this

11. Within a locality, you want to obtain the most income for the least capital used, i.e. compare the rental income from a 2-bed and the cost of the 2-bed, against a 3-bed

12. If you are considering flats, ensure that the long term property management will remain reasonable (lifts in a block of flats will cost money to maintain, especially as they get older), or that the price reflects these aspects.

As you can imagine there are a lot of pieces of information and data that need to be brought together and analysed before acceptable solutions are found from the thousands of property opportunities that are available. I liken this to a jigsaw puzzle; but ours has lots of pieces which can be joined in different ways depending on the picture we are trying to create. The way I complete the jigsaw puzzle is to gather all the data pieces I need and put them into Roly's Property Analyser (see Chapter 7).

I have shown you some of the basic strategies to create long term wealth and positive cash flow from investing in UK property. You now need to know 'how' to make this work in practice.

If you complete the puzzle correctly, your journey to financial freedom is perfectly achievable.

EXERCISE

Think about the type of investment property you might consider purchasing. Identifying what you do NOT want is just as important as indentifying what you DO want.

Some things to consider:

1. Do you want long term wealth creation, good cash flow or a combination?

2. Would you prefer property near where you live or elsewhere?

3. What sort of tenants might you want / not want?

4. Newly built property, older, no preference

5. Do you want to find the property yourself / use others?

6. Would you want to 'do-it-up' yourself / use others?

7. Would you want to look after the property yourself / use others?

PART III
Roly's Property Management System

Roly's Property Management System has several elements:

- Getting up to date information from trusted advisors and colleagues
- Roly's Property Analyser
- The 7 steps of the property investment process

In this part of the book I provide a step by step process that you will need to follow if you want to be a successful property investor. I start by telling you about the people and organizations involved in property so that you can become familiar about who does what. I talk generally about my Analyser, so you know what information you need in order to carry out a full and proper analysis of the properties, to ensure you only *buy the right property in the right location at the right price*. Then I take you through the process of buying, renting out and managing your investment property.

Even though I suggest that you use other people and organizations to do ALL or most of the process for you, I believe you need to understand what is involved.

I consistently keep in touch with the people I trust as advisors, because life doesn't stand still. I need to know what is new and what is changing, so that I can adapt my processes to suit. I will share with you the advisors I feel it is important for you to know about. You need to know that you are not alone. We all need to help each other to become successful.

I want to emphasise that I now work with people and organizations that are brilliant at undertaking all or most of the processes involved with property investing; from finding and financing a property to managing the tenant. If you do not want to make this another job for yourself, for whatever reason, you do not have to. You will be pleasantly surprised by the services you can obtain from others. Be warned though; you need to deal with the right people.

 In the next chapter I discuss the benefits of being a professional armchair investor, especially when you start out.

Roly's Property Analyser is a computerised system that I designed which ensures I only buy in Roly's Golden Zone. It helps me to make informed decisions about which property to buy; which one is best out of a selection and what my risk points are. It makes me think about and assess every step, from funding the purchase to refinance options: even before I make an offer on a property.

My 7 step property investment process has been developed since 2002 and is evolving all the time. It is especially important to keep up to date with legislation and to ensure that we comply fully with the law. It explains the sorts of things that Rachel and I do to buy and manage our properties. You will see that we have systemised the processes as much as we can, so that we know what to do; when to do it and how to do it.

CHAPTER 6
Advisors and support

Just like any other business; sport; or community you will need a support group around you to make things work more easily. You cannot build your wealth without the help of others. Some people or organizations will provide information; some will provide services and some will provide advice.

 There are many ways people make money from property. In this book I am teaching you about being 'a professional armchair investor'. Later, when you have had experience, or if you decide you want to make a career in the property arena, then you can take further training.

I want to help you *Retire Early Retire Wealthy* so I do not want to create another full time job for you.

Active Investor versus Professional Armchair Investor

Active Investor

An active investor is someone who does all or most of the following:

- Finds properties themselves
- Determines what work needs to be done
- Works out costs
- Knows the rental market and tenant's needs
- Knows the mortgage market
- Makes the decision whether to buy or not, based upon their criteria (I use Roly's Golden Zone and Roly's Property Analyser)
- Puts in place finance and mortgages
- Arranges the purchase
- Coordinates the work to prepare the property for tenants
- Organises the tenancy (refer to the Letting Agent section)
- Keeps up to date with the law and ensures continued compliance
- Maintains proper records and accounts
- KEEPS ON TOP OF THE MONEY
- Arranges refinancing when appropriate

As you can imagine, you need good systems and procedures to make this effective and efficient. It is possible to do all this alongside your current job but it does take commitment and a particular skill set.

Professional Armchair Investor

A professional armchair investor is someone who does all or most of the following:

• Understands what properties make a good investment (this book!)

• Seeks out an experienced mentor who provides independent support

• DECIDES which properties to buy, with the help of a mentor if necessary

• Looks after the buffer account

• Seeks out a person or organization that will do the following on their behalf:

- Offer suitable properties for purchase

- Provide financial guidance and support

- Help buy the property for you

- Manage the works, the tenancy and property maintenance

- Provide help and advice throughout,

- Deal with legislation changes for you

- Review the finances with you on a regular basis

- Provide you with records, accounts, etc

- PUT MONEY IN YOUR ACCOUNT

What does this mean?

For most people, running a portfolio of property themselves is either too time-consuming; too difficult; or simply too scary. Most people need support.

This is where I would like to help you. I know there are many people, just like I used to be, who would love to improve their financial situation, so that they can get on and enjoy their life, without worrying about their future.

I propose that you seriously consider being a professional armchair investor, at least for the time being. The next couple of chapters are a little more detailed and can appear overwhelming at first. So if you keep in the back of your mind that you can find someone you like and trust to 'do all this for you', then that is one concern removed.

The reason why I believe you need to know the information in this part of the book is so that you can see that investing in property, if done correctly, is supported by a collection of systematic processes, which help control your investment. Investing in property is not some chance happening, or hopeful gamble. The systems help minimise risk and maximise the upside potential.

Whether you become an armchair investor or an active one, you will mix with various people and organizations to some degree or another. You need to know that there is a support team and advisors around you and that you are not alone on your path to *Retire Early Retire Wealthy.* If you want to find out more about my advisors, then please let me know through the contact page of my website www.mylifesolutions.co.uk

Advisors, associations and companies related to property investment

The Independent Financial Advisor

Once you have decided that investing in property maybe suitable for you, then the first person you need to see is an Independent Financial Advisor (IFA).

Their role: to assess your current financial position and provide financial advice. Specifically they will inform you whether you can obtain a buy-to-let mortgage and if yes, tell you what your mortgage loan options are.

Finding an Independent Financial Advisor

When I was looking for my first property I did my own homework and had analysed the market options for buy-to-let mortgages. As I was visiting estate agents, I was invited to talk to their Financial / Mortgage Advisors. I was very disappointed, because the first 5 or 6 of them offered me buy-to-let products that did not seem to be better than the one I had found myself. Looking back, I don't think they really understood the buy-to-rent market.

They were simply offering me products from their company range.

After a few days, I met an IFA who was different to the rest. He found out about me and my financial circumstances and then used a computer system to identify what buy-to-let mortgage products were available to me. He told me what my various options were and provided advice and guidance and identified my preferences. After a short while, his computer system generated a list of products in order of my preference – and I was extremely amazed to see the product that I had found myself, at the top of his list!

It was now worth my while allowing him to apply for the mortgage on my behalf. I went back to him for my second property: he beat me that time; and I have trusted his company ever since. Nevertheless, I still test the market from time to time.

The word that made all the difference for me in the title 'Independent Financial Advisor' is 'Independent'. Many financial advisors are affiliated to a particular company that has products and services to sell. They can only recommend a mortgage product from a limited range. This means you are unlikely to get the best product that suits your need. An Independent Financial Advisor has the pick of (virtually) the whole market. This can be many thousands of products.

My IFA can advise you wherever you are in the country and wherever you want to buy.

Top Tip It is wise to use an IFA who has a track record of successful applications. You do not want to waste your time and application fees whilst the IFA takes 'a chance' on whether the proposed lender will accept you or the property. A good IFA knows the lenders criteria in depth and, if unsure, will phone them up to clarify issues before making the application.

The Conveyancing Solicitor

Your conveyancing solicitor needs to be experienced in buying and selling residential property. There will come a time when speed of purchase is really important. Your solicitor therefore needs to be one who will make that happen, rather than one who lets the process take its natural and, potentially, long-winded course. This will require them to be pro-active and practical. It goes without saying, they need to be accurate.

You should also 'shop around' to find a good combination of quality service and low fees.

The Legal Solicitor

Your legal solicitor must be someone who fully understands the relevant property laws; for example the Housing Act 2008 which has prescribed rules which must be adhered to, protecting both the Rights of the Tenant and the Rights of the Landlord.

They will help you through the legal system should you have problems with your property or your tenant.

Pursuing claims through the courts can be expensive so you

need to be aware of alternative places to seek advice and help to start with.

Landlord Associations

The National Landlord Association (is one of the largest recognised Associations)

If you are going to be letting and managing the properties yourself, then I suggest you join the National Landlord Association (NLA) because they will provide you with back up, advice relating to points of law, standard letter and form templates etc.

By joining the NLA, you can also take their free on-line course to become an Accredited Landlord, thus giving you credibility for your prospective tenants. My wife, Rachel, is accredited as she deals with the tenants on a regular basis and therefore needs to understand the latest information.

The Letting Agent

Finding a good letting agent is very important whilst you are building your property portfolio. You need to feel comfortable that they are going to look after you as the landlord as well as looking after your tenants. The extent of the services may vary from agent to agent and much will depend on what your own requirements are. Most letting agents will:

- Advise on the rent you can expect to receive
- Advertise and market your property
- Advise on presentation and furnishing of your property

- Advise on your responsibilities as a landlord
- Arrange safety checks and issue certificates as required
- Accompany viewings with prospective tenants
- Take up references and credit checks on prospective tenants
- Prepare and arrange the signing of the Tenancy Agreement
- Organise the inventory to be undertaken
- Collect the deposit from the tenant
- Lodge the deposit in accordance with tenancy deposit regulations (see the Deposit Protection Scheme below)
- Notify the Council Tax Office and utility companies of the change of occupier and the meters readings at the start and end of the tenancy
- Collect the monthly rent
- Forward payments to the landlord with statements
- Visit the property at regular intervals and provide a written report to the landlord
- Take responsibility for the day to day management of the property, arranging general repairs and maintenance etc
- Check out the tenant at the end of the tenancy and provide a report on condition to the landlord
- Organise the return of the deposit to the tenant

The majority of letting agencies will offer both letting only and full management services, but talk to several and negotiate and understand their terms before deciding which agent or agents to instruct.

Only use letting agents who are members of Association of Residential Letting Agents (ARLA) or similar.

The Deposit Protection Scheme

As part of the Housing Act 2004 the Government introduced tenancy deposit protection for all Assured Shorthold Tenancies (ASTs) in England and Wales where a deposit is taken.

You will need to ensure that the rules are followed, in terms of what information you need to provide to the tenant; protecting their deposit and complying with the prescribed times. Whilst you, as Landlord, are ultimately responsible, your letting agent should know all the rules and will be able to advise you; act for you and arrange for the deposit to be protected.

At the time of writing, there are 2 methods of protecting the deposit.

Custodial Scheme - where the deposit money is paid into a Government 'Authorised Scheme', such as the one provided by Deposit Protection Service (DPS).

Insured Scheme - where you hold the deposit money yourself and pay an insurance premium to a Government 'Authorised Scheme', such as My Deposits and Tenancy Deposit Scheme (TDS).

Top Tip Obtain copies of the paperwork associated with 'protecting' the deposit from your letting agent. You need to ensure that the deposit money is actually registered correctly and ONLY into a Government 'Authorised Scheme'. At the time of writing, there are only three authorised companies, as listed previously.

If the Landlord and Tenant cannot agree on the amount of deposit to be returned to the Tenant at the end of the tenancy, then the 'Authorised Scheme' will employ an independent arbiter who will look at all the evidence and make a binding decision.

If this is being administered on your behalf by a letting agent, then the letting agent should help you to provide suitable documentation and evidence.

The Mentor

A mentor is an experienced or knowledgeable person who helps to guide a less experienced, or less knowledgeable person. This form of help is often referred to as a mentorship and is more than just answering occasional questions, or providing ad hoc help. It is about an ongoing relationship of learning, dialogue, and challenge and entails informal communication, usually face-to-face and over a sustained period of time.

The focus of mentoring is to develop the whole person and so the techniques are broad and require wisdom in order to be used appropriately.

The way that a mentor can help less experienced people is by:

- Sowing the seeds of an idea where they feel the concept they are going to introduce is new and possibly inconceivable by the mentee (maybe this book!)
- Going through a process with the mentee
- Provoking a different way of thinking
- Showing examples of what they have done and the methods they use
- Encouraging the mentee to ask questions to clarify the learning points

The Property Finder (sourcing company)

There are people who specialise in finding properties that could be of interest to an investor. The property finder uses various techniques to find properties where vendors are willing to sell at a price below what other people in the street might find 'too low'. Once they find a potential property they will carry out the negotiations to agree a price and the necessary legal paperwork. The topic of finding these properties is a complete book in itself but it involves activities such as: on-line and off-line advertising campaigns, letter drops, regular liaison with estates agents and developers.

Often, the property finder will also arrange for any work to be done before selling the property onto another buyer. They make their money from property investors by charging a fee.

The advantage of using a property finder is that it saves an investor time and expense in travelling to all parts of the country searching for the best deals. They often have better negotiating skills and have a proven track record of following through on their promises to buy and so can buy property more cheaply than many people can. They can therefore frequently offer the property to an investor at a better price than the investor could achieve for themselves, even after allowing for the finder's fee.

The disadvantage is that you need to be careful who you trust as your property finder.

Top Tip

- Do not pay excessive fees before you actually make the purchase.

- Only use someone you can trust

- Past experience of a person is not a guarantee for next time

The Trainers

Once you know the fundamentals of property investing and you fully understand how the numbers work, you will be able to assess any property deal accurately and with confidence.

You may then feel that you want to be more 'hands-on'. You may want to do activities such as: finding property deals yourself in your locality; buying at auction; renting a house and sub-letting to others; buying a house for a pound; managing other people's property for good cash returns or joining an established franchise company.

There are lots of trainers that can help.

Top Tip

- Be careful not to try and do too many things at the same time. You will not succeed until you focus on one, maybe two, actions at any time until completion.

- Do not become a seminar junkie

- Most training companies teach only the latest fads or techniques that will only last a short period. These techniques are likely to work only in certain economic circumstances

- What you are being taught may not suit your personality. It may not work in your locality. You may not have the personal skills to make it work.

The all-encompassing organization

An all-encompassing organization is one that will become your mentor, your trainer, your property finder, your letting agent, your advisor and be there when you need them. They will help you identify your requirements from property investments and help you achieve YOUR dreams. They will help you to become a professional armchair investor – so that you can carry on with your life, with as little stress as possible.

Only work with someone you know, or someone who comes with strong recommendations and a proven track record. You need to feel you can trust them.

The Pension Advisor - in relation to property

After intensive investigation by a trusted colleague of mine, it has been established that it is now possible, legal and practical to be able to make use of your current pension fund to purchase residential property. If you have money sitting in a pension plan, you are now able to take out some of this money, invest it UK residential or commercial property and pay back your pension over time. If you believe that investing in UK property is something you wish to do and you have a pension pot that is not working hard for you, then this becomes an option for you to obtain a starting fund.

We have a word of warning though: please do not use the first organization that you happen to find. We are currently aware of only two companies, out of the many who have been scrutinised, that do this in a legal way.

The Tax Advisor and Will-Writer

I strongly advise you to seek advice from a tax advisor who thoroughly understands property. Ideally they will own their own property portfolio or advise landlords on regularly about their tax. They will be able to save you thousands of pounds if you meet them early.

The will-writer will help you with estate planning and set out your affairs in the way that suits you and your family needs, with a view of minimising the amount of taxes your estate would be due to pay.

These advisors will be able to:

- Assess your current and future incomes and liabilities
- Assist you with your current tax assessment
- Provide property tax advice
- Provide solutions to Inheritance Tax and Wills
- Make proposals on the most suitable way to structure your business, personal and property affairs

With regard to property, they will be able to advise you if it is best for you to buy as an individual; as partners; as tenants in common; in the name of a company and more. They will save you money.

Networking

Networking is an activity where like minded people get together to have discussions either as a full group, sub-groups or pairs. Ideas and stories are shared and everyone benefits from each other's experiences. Frequently people

arrange to meet outside the networking event so that they can get better acquainted and to explore ways in which they could work together for their mutual benefit – a 'joint venture'.

There are quite a few property networking events around the country and it is best to attend with a particular purpose in mind, but be open minded and do not judge people by their appearance.

Every successful person has a support team;

who will be in your team?

CHAPTER 7
Roly's Property Analyser

If you take a step back for a moment, you will notice that there is a lot of information you must take into account before making a purchase decision. Many people do not have the inclination, knowledge or skill to manage and analyse this amount of information themselves.

In order for me to manage my risks and ensure I only buy in Roly's Golden Zone, I need a robust system for gathering the relevant data and information; carrying out calculations and providing me with an analysis.

I am a Chartered Civil Engineer and I used to design buildings, bridges and roads using a variety of construction materials. I used to construct them and maintain them to pre-set monetary budgets and timescales. To do this I needed good analytical skills and excellent decision-making acumen. I also needed to understand managing money, forecasting, setting budgets, asset management, risk and performance management.

With this knowledge and skill set, I was able to create Roly's Property Analyser; which is a computerised system that I designed, to ensure that I only consider buying a property in Roly's Golden Zone. It helps me to make informed decisions about which property to buy; which one is best out of a selection and what my risk points are. It makes me think about and assess every step from funding the purchase to refinance options; even before I make an offer on a property.

The analyser includes items such as; purchase costs, works costs, mortgage costs, deposit borrowing costs, letting agent fees, contingencies, etc. By entering various bits of data, my analyser will let me know if a particular property is worth considering.

The purpose of Roly's Property Analyser is to determine whether a specific property meets certain criteria. If it does, then you can consider this property alongside other potential purchases. Finally, it can help identify which one of these works best for you.

Roly's Property Analyser is given to attendees of my one day workshop – "Roly's Road Map to Successful Property Investing" – where it is explained in detail. We look at real purchase opportunities and use my analyser to test if they meet our investment criteria.

Have a look at my website to find details of available workshops.

One of the most interesting observations is that virtually all the results you need, in order to understand whether a property is worth buying or not, can be calculated by knowing the price and the rent. As the rent is determined by the general market rent, the ONLY thing in your control is the purchase price.

Top Tip The only variable you really have the ability to influence - is the price you offer to buy the property for.

All the other numbers are pretty well fixed.

As an overview, the information you will need to know is:

Offer Price - The Offer Price is up to you: use the 'asking' prices as an indication of the 'Offer Price' but only make an offer if the numbers work. The asking price is simply the starting point at which the seller would like to sell. It is not necessarily the price they would actually sell at. If calculated analysis suggests that this property is an option, the Offer Price is the only number you can 'play with' to get the most appropriate purchase deal. All the other numbers are pretty well fixed!

The likely value of the property once you have done any improvement - you need to know this so that you can work out if you stand a reasonable chance of taking all, or most, of your own money back out in the near future.

Likely growth of the property market - you need to understand whether the property you are considering to buy will rise in value and by how much. The deeper you delve into the statistics the more likely you are to understand the market place and the potential growth rate.

The rent - the rental value for mortgage purposes will be determined by the lender's surveyor, who will provide a RICS valuation report to the lender. The surveyor's view will be influenced by the rent currently being achieved by similar properties in the locality and by a judgement whether that rent is sustainable in the economic climate at that time. The actual rent you obtain may be different and will be determined by the demand for your property at the time you are looking for a tenant. You can look on the internet, e.g. www.rightmove.co.uk or speak with a local letting agent. Then use this as your best guess of the rental value when undertaking a property analysis.

The mortgage products available – various mortgage types are discussed in Chapter 8 Step1. Each product is going to give a different result. Work with an IFA to indentify the most suitable options. You might end up with 2 or 3 products with varying 'Loan to Value' percentages; Interest rates; tie-in periods; arrangement fees etc. Then enter the data into Roly's Property Analyser to assess the effect of all the products' variables for each property you are considering.

Other costs and potential expenses – information about these can be found mainly in Chapter 8.

The results you will obtain

Roly's Property Analyser will produce the results that will provide you with sufficient information for you to make informed decisions about whether to buy a property or not. The output information is:

- Maximum allowable mortgage
- Monthly cost of the mortgage
- Deposit needed
- Professional and Legal costs to purchase the property
- Cost of "getting the property ready to rent"

- Total amount of your own money needed

- Monthly and annual running costs

- Does it give positive Cash Flow?

- Does it give a better Return on Investment than current savings? (i.e. how much cash return do you get for parting with £xx of your cash employed)

- When will you be likely to refinance it, to take all or most of your money back out?

- Will it still give positive cash flow after refinancing?

Secondary checks

There are two further checks I occasionally make, to determine if one property is a better option than another. They are 'Return on Investment' (ROI) and 'Yield'. There are a lot of complications around the measurement of both of these indicators and so I only use them as a means to compare a few similar investment opportunities once I know the opportunity is good.

Return on Investment

Return on Investment is a simple concept but has different methods of calculation. I believe that if you are consistent in your approach, then it will give you a good idea of the relative merits of each property you are considering.

Return on Investment = Annual Net Income divided by the Cash Employed x100

Cash Employed is the amount of your own money you have to part with to buy the property and get it ready for renting.

Net income is your rental income less all of your running expenses

Example of Return on Investment		
Property purchase price		£96,000
Your Cash Employed (including deposit, costs and refurb)		£28,000
Monthly income after expenses	£200	
Annual Net Income	£2,400	
ROI = 2,400/28,000 x 100 =		8.6%

Yield

Yield = Annual Gross Rent divided by Purchase Price

In our experience, you get a better return for your money and a better yield if you buy a one or two bedroom property. This is because the rental income you get from these types of properties, as a proportion of the purchase price, is generally higher than for larger single let properties i.e. you get a higher Yield.

Example of Yield		
Property purchase price		£96,000
Monthly income before expenses	£600	
Annual Gross Rent	£7,200	
Yield = 7,200/96,000 x 100 =		7.5%

In order to become a professional property investor, you need a proven system to guide you to take appropriate and effective action.

CHAPTER 8
The 7 steps of the property investment process

The 7 steps of the property investment process are:

1. Funding your property purchase

2. Purchasing the property

3. Getting the property ready to rent

4. Setting up and managing the tenancy

5. Maintaining the property

6. Record keeping: legal compliance; tax; and accounting

7. Reviewing the property value and refinancing

Chapter 8 - Step 1:
Funding your property purchase

The mortgage product and finding your deposit

One of the reasons why UK property is such a good investment opportunity is because of the way buy-to-let mortgages operate. You can borrow money from someone else and make it work to your benefit. You should use an 'interest only' mortgage, as described below, so you do not need to pay back the borrowed money until sometime way into the future. You do not even need income from a salary to be able to borrow in this way, although you have more options if you do.

Alongside the mortgage, you will need some money to use as a deposit and to pay for the purchase expenses. Later on we can investigate where your money might come from.

The funds to purchase your investment property will come from two primary sources:

- Buy-to-let mortgage
- Your own funds

Top Tip This is the time you will need to speak to your Independent Financial Advisor (IFA).

Buy-to-let mortgages

Although your IFA will go through buy-to-let mortgages with you, I would like to give you some information to help you understand how they work.

The significant aspects of the mortgage are:

Interest-only or repayment mortgages

Unlike the majority of residential buyers, the buy-to-let investor generally takes out an **interest-only** mortgage. This means that you only pay off the interest on the money borrowed each month and don't pay off any capital. Because of this, the monthly payments are lower and this helps improve cash flow. This method works because you could sell the investment property to pay back the loan if needed.

You cannot do this easily with your main residence.

In addition, in the early years of the investment you are trying to maximise the capital growth so paying it back through a repayment mortgage goes against the initial ethos.

When you have several properties and are approaching an 'exit' or 'retirement' position, it may be wise to look at paying off some of the mortgage debt to give higher regular income. This needs very careful handling when that time comes, and thorough analysis will be required.

Fixed rate or variable rate

Mortgages with **fixed rates** are set so that you pay the same interest rate and therefore the same amount of money each month for a particular specified time; anything between one and five years. After the period of the fixed rate, the mortgage normally reverts to the lender's **standard variable rate**.

Mortgages with **variable rates** specify that the rate of interest you pay is a specified percent in addition to a particular 'base rate'. For example it could be 2% over Bank of England base rate. This means that the amount you pay each month is variable depending upon the Bank of England base rate.

It is difficult to predict what will happen with interest rates – but with the help of your IFA, you will come to a view on what type is best for you at any particular moment. When you have several properties, it is prudent to have a mixture of both 'fixed rate' and 'variable rate' interest mortgages.

Tie-in period / overhang period

The **tie-in period** is normally the length of time that your 'special' or 'introductory' rate offer is based upon. The **tie-in period** can be between one and five years.

Beware though that some products also tie you in for a longer period than the special offer. This is called an **overhang**. You are committed to the tie-in of the promotional period when you will be charged the special offer rate, plus a time - maybe one or two years - at the lender's rate. The lender's rate is normally more expensive than the special rate. Try to avoid these overhang mortgages.

Early redemption charge

Most mortgage products will have an **early redemption charge**: this is payable to the lender, if you decide to repay the mortgage loan before the tie-in period has been completed. This is normally expensive and therefore you need to be fully committed to your strategy before agreeing to long tie-in periods. You are unlikely to want to pay the charges - which could be as much as 6% of the loan. So, for a £100,000 mortgage loan you would pay an **early redemption charge** of £6,000.

Bank of England Base Rate / Libor / Lenders Standard Variable Rate

Most lenders will make their special offers based upon Bank of England (BoE) Base Rate. This rate is determined by the Bank of England once a month and this is the interest rate that most people are familiar with.

Some lenders use the London Interbank Offered Rate (Libor). This is the rate of interest that banks pay one another when borrowing money from each other. It is the banks' borrowing rate. The Libor associated with a mortgage will be reviewed at intervals set by the lender and the interest rate is often a small percentage higher than BoE rate.

The **Libor** is the average interest rate that leading banks in London charge, when lending to other banks. It is an acronym for **London Interbank Offered Rate (LIBOR)**

Banks borrow money for one day, one month, two months, six months, one year, etc., and they pay interest to their lenders based on certain rates. The Libor figure is an average of these rates.

It is more important that you chose the right product than that worry about which particular rate the product is attached to.

The lender's **Standard Variable Rate** is a rate that the lender would like you to borrow the money at. It is often more expensive than the special offers. A few months before the end of the special offer period, it is best for your IFA to review what other products are available and switch accordingly.

Arrangement fee

When you take out a mortgage you will pay an arrangement fee, often based upon a percentage of the borrowed amount. It could be anything from around £500 to £4000. This fee can generally be added to the loan, but you will pay interest on it each month. You pay it off in full at the end of the loan period.

It is best to add it to the loan rather than using your own precious capital at the buying stage. Pay it off at the end when you are 'in the money' or are remortgaging.

Survey fee

The lender will want to do a survey of the property to check that it is suitable to lend against. The fee will be around £300 to £500 and is usually payable by the applicant up-front and is not refundable.

Once your IFA puts in your application forms, the survey is one of the first things the lender does.

This survey is not for your benefit and you are unlikely to get the full results.

If you are in any doubt about the condition of the property you intend to buy, you should consider getting a survey done yourself.

Mortgage criteria

Unlike normal residential mortgages, some lenders do not require a minimum income from you, although you will have more choice of products if you do have another income.

It is also worth noting that you **DO NOT** have to own your own home to borrow from some lenders in order to purchase your buy-to-let property, although you may need to be recognised as an 'experienced' landlord. So there is a possibility to 'joint venture' with an experienced landlord, to get your foot on the investment ladder.

The buy-to-let mortgage is a great product because it is not affected by any other borrowing you may have. A word of warning though, the lender will be checking the amount of credit and debt you have, together with your credit rating.

It is best to check with your mortgage advisor early in the process to evaluate what will be your likely borrowing capability.

As the lender will be checking your credit report through a company like Experian, it might be worth you doing this yourself first so you can talk about it with your independent financial advisor.

Lenders have two criteria for calculating the maximum they will lend to you. The final offer they will make to you will be based upon the lowest of:

- Loan to Value (LTV)

- Predicted rental income (as supplied by the lender's surveyor) combined with their multiplier on rent income

The information below, provided by the lender, is the sort of data you require to assess whether this product will work for the particular property you are considering

MORTGAGE INFORMATION	
Max Loan to Value	75%
Product type	2 year fixed
Tie-in period	2 years
Interest rate (for the 2 year tie-in period)	4.35%
multiplier on rent income	125%
arrangement fee (added to loan)	2.50%

Maximum loan based upon purchase price

Each mortgage product will have a specific maximum Loan to Value ratio that they will lend. A 75% Loan to Value means that the maximum they will lend is 75% of the purchase price or the RICS valuation, whichever is the lower. So for a £96,000 property the loan could be up to £72,000.

At the time of writing, the Loan to Value % can be anything between 65% and 85%.

MAXIMUM LOAN BASED ON PURCHASE PRICE		
Purchase price		£96,000
Loan to Value ratio (LTV)	75%	
Max Mortgage = price x LTV =		£72,000

Maximum loan based upon rental income

Lenders also check that the annual rental value exceeds the amount of mortgage payments you need to make by 125% to 130% (their 'safety factor' multiplier on rent income). The mortgage payments are calculated by multiplying the amount being borrowed by the 'pay rate'. The pay rate is generally the same as the interest rate but not always.

MAXIMUM LOAN BASED ON RENTAL VALUE	
RICS monthly rental value	£600
Predicted annual rent	£7,200
Annual rent divided by Safety Factor is	
£7200/1.25 =	£5,760
Max loan (rent) = £5760 / pay rate of 4.35%	
Max loan (rent) =	£132,414

The Maximum Loan

The maximum the lender will offer you is lowest of the two calculations. In this case £72,000 based upon LTV.

MAXIMUM LOAN	
Max Mortgage = price x LTV =	£72,000
Max Mortgage (rent) =	£132,414
Max Mortgage is therefore	**£72,000**

Mortgage payment

The cost to borrow this mortgage is calculated by adding the arrangement fee to the mortgage and multiplying by the interest rate.

This gives the annual amount of interest due. Divide by 12 to arrive at your monthly payments. If you are on a fixed rate, this is the amount you will pay for the duration of the product; in this case 2 years. After 2 years it will revert to the lender's standard variable rate.

COST OF MORTGAGE	
Mortgage Loan	£72,000
Arrangement Fee is 2.5% of Loan = 2.5 x 72,000/100 =	£1,800
TOTAL Loan	**£73,800**
The interest payable for the first 2 years is:	
4.35% x £73,800 per annum = £3,210	
So, Interest per month is	**£267.53**

Funding the deposit

Your IFA will require you to demonstrate that you have the deposit money. The deposit is the difference between the price you are paying for the property less the mortgage loan, i.e. £96,000 take away £72,000 = £24,000.

In practice though, you will need to find £28,000 because there are expenses; in this example £4,000.

INITIAL COSTS		
Buy the property - price		£96,000
Legal costs		£2,000
Add Value (do work)		£2,000
TOTAL COSTS		**£100,000**
FUNDED BY		
75% Mortgage	£72,000	
The remainder of the money needed will come from own funds	£28,000	
TOTAL USED	**£100,000**	

Where can I find this money?

There are several ways that you could find this money:

a) From your current savings

b) From your current investments

- You should ensure that the income generated from your new investment property is going to be greater than the income generated from your current savings and investments: unless you are primarily investing to create long term wealth, in which case a break-even outcome may be acceptable to you. Roly's Property Analyser takes this into account.

c) Releasing equity from your home

- Releasing equity from your own home is basically remortgaging your home to take more money out. Your IFA will be able to advise you on this.

RELEASING EQUITY FROM YOUR HOME	
Home value	£250,000
Current mortgage	£100,000
Refinance to new mortgage (65% loan to value)	£162,500
Equity released	**£62,500**

- The way to assess whether releasing equity from your home is a good choice is to ensure that the income generated from the new investment property is going to be greater than the cost of:
  - Mortgage payments for the investment property
  - Running costs of the investment property, and
  - Additional cost of borrowing the money against your home

- In other words, only do this if the numbers work [Roly's Property Analyser]

- The great news is that the costs incurred due to borrowing money to finance your investment property, are allowable expenses, which can be offset against your income when calculating your tax liabilities.

d) Borrowing money from others

- There are options of borrowing money from family, friends and colleagues.

- The best way might be to work with your immediate family. One idea could be for them to remortgage their home. You would cover all costs including the cost of the additional borrowing. You could even give them a little more but this is up to you.

- When borrowing cash, you would need to draw up an agreement about repayment of interest and funds and to provide some guarantee that the money would be repaid.

- You can offer to pay a specific amount of interest each month and a typical percentage is anything from 5% per year to 10% per year, but the amount is really dependent on what you believe is fair. It would need to be more than the rate your family / friend lender is currently achieving and would potentially achieve for the period in question.

e) Borrowing money from your pension

- You read earlier in Chapter 6 that it may be possible to borrow money from your current pension. If you have pensions and would like to know more about releasing this money to invest in property, then let me know through the contact page of my website www.mylifesolutions.co.uk . I will put you in touch with trusted professionals, who will, in my opinion, provide you with a service which will truly look after your best interests.

EXERCISE

Consider how much deposit you could raise by yourself

You will need to gather information about your current circumstances and your future plans, such as:

How much deposit can you raise?	
Asset	**£**
Equity in your home	
Equity from any current investments	
Savings	
Pension	
Sum of Assets	
Liabilities	**£**
Current liabilities	
Known or expected large expenses	
Sum of Liabilities	
Net Asset Value (Net Worth) = Assets - Liabilities	**£**

Your Independent Financial Advisor will be able to help you calculate your 'available deposit' and the information listed above will help enormously so that the IFA can fully understand your position.

I have a template on the website you could use to collate this information.

EXERCISE

Consider how much deposit you could raise with others

If you feel that you may not have funds to use as a deposit at the moment, consider who might be willing to 'believe in you' and lend you some money. Do not approach them until you have a specific plan written down with compelling reasons for investing in you and why your plan will work.

How much deposit can you raise with others?	
Person	**£**
Total	

Allocation of your cash – your strategy for investing

Use of your cash

Now that you have identified how much capital money you could find for investment purposes, you will need to decide how best to use these funds.

This will be allocated as follows:

- Fund the deposit
- Paying to carry out works
- Put aside some money into your Property Buffer Account.

Your Property Buffer Account

 You should put between 5% and 10% of the property value into your Property Buffer Account.

This will be available to use should any significant unforeseen costs arise, such as replacing a boiler. It is better to have this pot in place as a contingency measure, than to be worrying about 'what if ... things don't go to plan'. The buffer removes the worry and you can get on with your life, hopefully stress free.

How long will my Property Buffer last?

Let's say your property is valued at £200,000 and financed with a £50,000 deposit and a £150,000 mortgage. You put £15,000 into your buffer account and this is equivalent to 7.5% of your property value.

If the mortgage rate goes up by an additional 4%, you will need to pay an additional amount each year equivalent to £150,000 x 4% = £6,000.

We have found the most expensive item for 'general maintenance' has been replacing a boiler. Allow £3,000.

The buffer of £15,000 covers these items adequately.

Evaluating your investment options

Once you have worked out how much you can afford to invest, you now need to evaluate what would be the best investment strategy for you to achieve **your Goal**.

To give you a broad idea of what might be achievable, let's look at a few basic scenarios. If you have:

Less than £5,000

Earn some extra cash. If you need help in creating an investment pot, you will find more information in Chapter 10 and by going to my website.

Less than £20,000

 If you have less than £20,000 you will probably need to do some joint ventures in order to get enough working capital to buy solely in your own name. For example, you could join a 'joint investment fund' where like-minded people have a share in the investment. This must be professionally managed and is a legal arrangement enforceable by a court of Law.

Over £20,000

If you have between £20,000 and £50,000 you can invest in property but you may be restricted from some expensive locations.

Over £50,000

If you have between £50,000 and £150,000 most of the strategies will be open to you and you will have some really great opportunities; buy one large property in a select locality or a few in other areas.

You should consider if you have any preferences: newer properties; one, or multiple properties; nearby or in some other location – maybe a specific part of the UK; in a city, or in the countryside? If you do have preferences, you can narrow the search down to your requirements. If not, you will need more time to evaluate all your options.

Over £150,000

If you have over £150,000 to invest, then buying either a property in London or another high growth location, or a high cash flowing HMO would be good options.

London property has the advantage of great long term growth and good cash flow; **providing you buy the right property**. Even with the instability in the housing market over the past couple of years, London has not really seen reductions in house values. For this reason I would suggest that you will be able refinance this type of property more quickly than most other places in the country.

An HMO gives really good cash flow, as explained in Chapter 4, so you would be able to pay other people to manage it for you and still get a very good return on your money. The location of the HMO would depend upon exactly how much you have to invest and whether you want the HMO to be for students, housing benefit clients or single accommodation for young professionals. There are prescribed rules and regulations regarding HMOs and these are enacted to different degrees by local authorities across the country. For this reason, I cannot go into all the detail in this book. The ways the regulations are applied changes frequently. If HMOs interest you, I suggest you learn how to apply the fundamentals of property investing first and then I can advise you further. For example, I can introduce you to an excellent HMO franchise company.

Chapter 8 - Step 2: Purchasing the property

The purchase process is quite straightforward:

1. Make an offer – generally through a selling agent

2. Engage a solicitor to make the purchase

3. Ask your mortgage advisor to submit your mortgage application. They will also need to see proof of deposit funds.

4. Once the offer has been approved and your solicitor has agreed with you that everything is acceptable, you are in a position to proceed

5. Optional – confirm with your letting agent that you are buying and they should start to get the details ready to market the property.

6. Give your deposit to your solicitor and they will exchange contracts

7. Optional – inform your letting agent that they can now market the property

8. Take out relevant insurances prior to exchange

9. Exchange and Completion often takes place on the same date for buy-to-let purchases, but it does not have to.

Your Independent Financial Advisor

Your IFA should work closely with your solicitor to ensure your purchase goes smoothly. Your IFA will complete the mortgage application with you and send it to the lender for approval. The IFA may make a charge for this. You will be required to pay the lender for them to carry out a survey of the property you wish to mortgage.

Once the mortgage has been approved and the solicitor has carried out the necessary searches etc and is satisfied everything is in order, you are ready to proceed with the purchase.

Estimate of Mortgage Application Costs	
IFA	£350
Mortgage Survey	£400
Mortgage Application Costs	**£750**

Your Conveyancing Solicitor

Before you engage a solicitor they will give you a quotation for acting on your behalf. The quote will give you an estimation of costs your solicitor needs to pay out on your behalf and the fees which they charge.

Solicitor Purchase Costs	
Solicitor Fees	£500
Stamp Duty*	£0
Solicitor Purchase Costs	**£500**

*Stamp Duty is a tax payable to the Government and the amount varies depending upon the 'tax rules' of the day. See http://www.hmrc.gov.uk/sdlt/intro/rates-thresholds.htm

Other Ancillary Expenses and Contingencies

Void Periods

There will be a period between the date of purchase and the date of your first tenant when your investment property will be empty. From experience, you should allow 6 weeks without rent.

In your calculations therefore, you should allow for paying a mortgage for 6 weeks without receiving any rent.

Finder's Fee

If you use someone else to help you find a property for you, then you will need to add their fee into your calculations to ensure you have worked out how much cash you need.

Property Building and Contents Insurance

You will need your prospective property to be insured, for the minimum amount specified in the lender's valuation report, from the day that you exchange contracts.

If you purchase a Leasehold property then the building should be insured by the lease holder. Your solicitor will need to check this out for you.

You will also need 'contents' cover even if your rental property will be unfurnished. It is best to be covered for 'accidental and malicious damage by the tenant' as well as covering damage to your property. This should also cover you for third party injury, damage by fire and theft.

You should be able to pay for this in monthly instalments.

Chapter 8 - Step 3: Getting the property ready to rent

There are two aspects to consider when getting your property to rent:

- Minimum requirements
- Additional work

Minimum requirements

You will need to plan to do the following things:

Condition

1. The property will need to be up to a standard expected by the tenant in that location, for the rent you are going to charge. Your letting agent will advise you on the initial condition you need to achieve for your target audience. (They could also arrange for the gas and electric checks, the Energy Performance Certificate (EPC) and inventory to be carried out for you)

2. I would suggest that the property needs to be clean and tidy and it is essential that all equipment is in good working order.

3. Carry out any minor repair work

Health and Safety and other Legal Requirements

4. You are required to have a Landlords Gas Safety Certificate if the property is supplied with gas. You need to employ a **Gas Safe** registered engineer who will carry out the necessary checks and issue you with the certificate. This must be renewed every 12 months.

5. At the time of writing this book, an electrical safety check is not mandatory, but there is a legal duty upon the landlord to carry out risk assessments. Part of this requirement is that you consider the electrical safety. If the property is old, appears run down or has plug sockets and wires visible on the surface of the walls rather than within, I suggest you get an electrical safety check done. We normally work on the basis that we will generally not undertake an electrical safety check if the property is less than 10 years old. Older than that, we assess when an inspection would be appropriate. When one has been done, we ask the assessing engineer to recommend when the next check should take place.

6. You will need a Portable Appliance Test (PAT) certificate for each portable appliance (one with a plug) that is in the property if you are unsure of the plugs' integrity.

7. You will need an Energy Performance Certificate (EPC) which shows how the property performs in relation to energy efficiency. You can use the one issued to you when you bought the property. Currently it should be renewed after 10 years.

8. Record your risk assessment just in case a tenant has an accident and decides it is your fault.

Insurance

9. Part of your mortgage requirement is that you have to hold building insurance cover. I strongly recommend that you take out a specific Landlord's building and contents insurance policy that includes cover for malicious and accidental damage by the tenant. Build this into your cash flow calculations.

Inventory and its importance

10. You will need an inventory of the property to be carried out. An inventory is a schedule setting out the condition of the property. This is needed even if the property does not have any furniture in it, because it includes walls, flooring, all decoration, cleanliness, inside and out, and more. It lists everything at the property and gives each item a condition statement. It must be written and can be supplemented by photographs and / or a video.

On the day the tenant moves in, they are given a copy of the inventory which they must sign to agree. This is the starting condition of the tenancy. At the end, this will be checked off to ensure the tenant has caused no damage.

The basic premise is that the tenant must leave the property in a condition no worse than when the tenancy started. Any shortfall in condition is to be paid for by the tenant, and costs 'reasonably' incurred can be deducted from the tenant's deposit. Remember that the tenant must sign to agree that any rectification jobs can be carried out at their expense.

You must, as the Landlord, accept fair wear and tear during a tenancy period. For example carpets will get worn by general use.

The inventory effectively limits your liability for damage by the tenant.

Costs associated with getting the property ready to rent: Initial One-off	
Minor repair work, estimate	£160
Landlord Gas Safety Certificate	£70
Electrical PAT testing (optional)	£40
EPC (included with purchase)	
Inventory	£80
Insurance	£220
TOTAL set-up COSTS	**£570**

Additional work

You may wish to do further work along the lines that I suggested earlier in the book.

Cost of additional work	
Changing windows, say	£1,600
Other	£0
Total add-on COSTS	**£1,600**

Chapter 8 - Step 4: Setting up and managing the tenancy

This process could be given in whole or in part to a letting agent who will charge you a fee, generally based upon a percentage of the rental income. They may also charge you some fees up front to cover finding a tenant.

Costs associated with letting and managing your property

The costs associated with letting and managing your property will depend on whether you do it yourself or engage a letting agent to do it for you. Their charges vary from agent to agent and town to town.

For the purposes of Roly's Property Analyser, allow 10% of the monthly rent plus VAT.

The letting agent will collect the rent on your behalf, deduct their fees plus any 'maintenance' costs they have paid on your behalf and send you the remainder of the money a few days later.

Monthly costs associated with letting and managing your property		
Income from Rent		£600
Letting Agent Costs (monthly)	£60	
VAT	£12	
Total Letting Agent fees	**£72**	
Maintenance in month	£0	
Total Deductions	£72	
Amount Credited to your bank		**£528**

The letting agent's job

If you are new to property investing, then I would strongly advise you to use an Association of Registered Letting Agents (ARLA) accredited letting agent, or team up with someone who has a track record of managing their own properties successfully. As you will remember from the list of letting agent jobs set out in Chapter 6, it is quite an extensive subject and for that reason I will only describe the main elements in this book.

A letting agent should do all the things detailed in the list in Chapter 6. You will need to look through their company's particular terms and conditions to familiarise yourself with the exact service you can expect from them, before you engage them.

The sequence of events for setting up and managing the tenancy is along the lines as follows:

Find a tenant

You may be charged a fee by the agent for finding a tenant in addition to the monthly management fee.

Vet the tenant

All tenants will be credit checked and other references will be sought in an attempt to ensure they are likely to be good tenants and good payers.

If the prospective tenant generally appears good, but there is some doubt - perhaps their financial position is not as good as you would want - then they may be asked for a Guarantor. A Guarantor is normally a family member or close friend of the prospective tenant, who effectively underwrites the tenancy agreement and will have to sign to say that they will ensure the tenancy agreement is fulfilled. If the tenant defaults in some way then the Guarantor will be liable. The Guarantor should be checked in the same way as the prospective tenant.

All persons over 18 years old who will be living at the property must be listed as a tenant on the Agreement.

Draw up the tenancy agreement and agree the tenancy period

The prospective tenant will agree the moving-in date and the length of the tenancy. All this information, plus the terms of the tenancy will be recorded in a legal document called an Assured Shorthold Tenancy Agreement (AST).

We recommend that you offer the minimum period allowed for an Assured Shorthold Tenancy Agreement which is 6 months. This allows you time to fully get to know your tenant before offering them a longer contract. This would normally be for 12 months.

Top Tip We have found that leading up to Christmas is a time when many people do not want to change homes. Letting your property becomes more difficult at this time. So, if a tenancy would normally be due for renewal in November to January, consider offering them a 9 month tenancy instead of a 6 month one in order to avoid changing tenants during the winter period

Pre-tenancy checks

The prospective tenant should see a copy of the Assured Shorthold Tenancy Agreement that you intend to use so they can read through it before the start date without any pressure.

You have a legal responsibility to ensure you have all the Health and Safety and other legal paperwork in place as described in Step 3.

An inventory will be carried out by an independent inventory clerk.

Showing the tenant in

- The first month's rent and the deposit will be collected from the tenant.

- The tenant will complete a standing order form for future monthly payments.

- The tenant will be shown into the property

- The deposit money will be registered with a Deposit Protection Scheme within legal time frames.

- The energy suppliers and Council Tax Office will be informed about the tenant, start date and meter readings.

Manage the tenant and the property during the tenancy

The letting agent will inspect the property on your behalf at regular intervals to check that the property is being looked after in the way it should be.

They will provide you with a written report and discuss any issues with you.

Review the rent

You are able to review the rent at the outset of every new tenancy agreement or after each 12 months of a Periodic Tenancy.

A tenancy agreement becomes a Periodic Tenancy when the original agreement period has been exceeded by mutual agreement.

A Periodic Tenancy works for both parties if the tenant:

- is not sure about their job prospects
- is thinking about upsizing or downsizing
- has a job that may require them to move at any time
- has lost some income and this becomes a concern to you

Termination of the tenancy agreement including check-out

You should ensure that your letting agent reviews the tenancy two months prior to end of the tenancy agreement to learn if the tenant is intending to stay or leave. Either way they can begin to either start advertising or draw up a new AST.

When the AST is terminated your letting agent will, on the day the tenant leaves, check the condition of the property against the original inventory. The agent will send you a report on condition and discuss with you how much of the deposit, if any, should be withheld.

Chapter 8 - Step 5: Maintaining the property

Property maintenance issues will be dealt with by your letting agent who will discuss these with you and obtain quotes on your behalf.

It is always best to deal with any problems promptly. The tenant will appreciate this and be more likely to stay with you and be more forgiving if something doesn't go according to plan.

If you decide to manage the property yourself, you will need to carry out regular inspections and be 'on-call' if the tenant has any problems.

You should build a list of tradesmen you know and can trust. This may be difficult in the early days. If you know a landlord or a friendly letting agent, then they will be able to help you with a name. You will need a plumber, gas engineer, electrician and an odd-job man, preferably two of each. Other tradesmen can be found as needed, and once found, added to your list.

It is best to build up a trusting relationship with your tradesmen. This means that sometimes you may need to leave decisions to them when fixing a job, rather than reporting back to you. Allow them to make decisions within agreed parameters. This will save time and ultimately save money. Once a job is done and you receive their invoice, pay it straight away. Do not leave it to the last minute. They will know that you always pay quickly and will put themselves out for you when you have an urgent job.

I have also found that the cheapest is not necessarily the best. These tradesmen are often very busy so may not be able to 'fit you in' when you need them. Some are looking to do a quick job and get out. I have a very good plumber who is not necessarily the cheapest, but is reasonable, and I get a great service.

A great team player – my plumber

I know we can trust him in a house when no-one is in (although it is best to get the tenant's agreement first). He will turn up when agreed and provide excellent service and advice.

I have called him on several occasions 'out-of-hours'. Once was around 10pm on a Saturday because the tenant arrived home from holiday to find water coming through the ceiling! On the phone, he talked through what I needed to do to stop the flow of water (from the central heating pump) and stayed on the line until I was satisfied.

He agreed to come the following day, Sunday, at 9.30am to sort it out. His out-of-hours rate is the same as his normal rate for me – an amazing benefit.

I'm not sure he even charged for the 15 minutes on the phone Saturday evening. Brilliant!

Don't forget to keep all invoices, receipts and records of correspondence with the tenant safely in your filing system (Step 6).

Property running costs are made up of:

- Minor maintenance
- Gas certificates
- Insurance
- Ground rent (for leasehold properties)
- Building Maintenance Fees (for flats)
- Grounds Maintenance Fees (for flats and some new estates)

Ongoing annual running costs	
Maintenance, allow 3% of annual rent	£216
Landlord Gas Safety Check	£70
Insurance	£220
Freehold / Grounds maintenance	£0
Annual running COSTS	**£506**

Contingency - Void periods

I calculate the void period percentage based upon the

property being vacant for two weeks per year equivalent to 4% per annum. If you buy the right property in the right location, then 4% is more than enough – but I like to be prudent, so this is the number I use.

You will notice over time that the void period becomes less and less and gets almost to the point when *you* can dictate the empty period between tenants; for example, to allow you to do some work on the property.

Contingency	
Void period, allow 4% of annual rent (equivalent to around 2 weeks per year)	£288
Allowance for Contingencies	**£288**

Chapter 8 - Step 6: Record keeping; legal compliance; tax and accounting

Record keeping

For some people keeping records and accounting may not be very inspiring. For some, this may be your forte. Whatever your take on this, it is an essential task to perform; not least because you will need to produce accounts for tax purposes.

If the filing and record keeping is done correctly and accurately as an ongoing activity, then you can find things instantly thus saving time; enabling you to deflect or contest accusations by tenants and ensuring that all money is accounted for and that you are legally compliant.

There is Data Protection legislation you will need to comply with when keeping tenants' and prospective tenants' personal records. You will find guidance at www.ico.gov.uk

The filing system

There are different levels of filing systems required to manage your property investment business. This is the way we have compiled our own filing system.

Summary of Accounts

The purpose of this file is to pull together all aspects of your finances so that your tax return can be completed efficiently and effectively. You will need a spreadsheet and a hard copy of your summary pages. This will include a summary of all your investment properties.

Cash Flow

The purpose of this file is to ensure that your forecast cash flow remains on track. You will check your monthly income and expenses are as expected. You will re-forecast your cash flow with every change. You will do this monthly as a minimum. This spreadsheet is not solely confined to your investment properties as it should also include your personal income and expenditure.

Accountant and Tax

The purpose of this file is to record what information you have given to both your accountant or tax advisor and the tax office. Keep ALL receipts.

It will reduce your accountant's fee if you compile a detailed spreadsheet for them to check against. Keep all correspondence in this file. Your accountant will help you with both your annual tax returns and your capital gain returns.

Remember I mentioned earlier that your tax advisor will be able to provide good tax planning advice if you talk to them early enough.

A second part of this file will be recording the information you give to and receive from the tax office.

Financial Advisor

The purpose of this file is to record what information you have given to and received from your financial advisor. This could also include liaison with your investment property advisor.

From time to time you will review the whole of your investment property portfolio and other investments, with your advisor. This will include a summary of current property values, mortgages and cash flows. You will assess the possibility of refinancing your properties.

When you apply for refinance or a new mortgage you will require key pieces of information to hand. This file is the place where you keep this information.

Past Tenancies

The purpose of this file is to keep an archive of all previous tenancy details. This file will need an index page. You should keep old records in case anyone decides to challenge you later about any aspect of their time with you. Remember to comply with Data Protection legislation.

Specific Property Filing System

For *EACH* property you will require *several* hard copy files

- Solicitor (purchase documents including deeds and selling documentation including capital gains return)

- Mortgage (applications, offers, terms and conditions, statements, etc and this file include any previous ones if you refinance)

- Letting agent (terms and conditions; correspondence; invoices; receipts for work)

- Current tenancy (AST agreements; Deposit Registration; inventory; tenants' contact details; Landlords Gas Safety Certificate; PAT certificates; EPC; inspection reports; record of maintenance issues and correspondence with tenants; tenants' original references and credit checks; appliance instructions; guarantor agreement and their details, if applicable). Your letting agent should supply you with copies of these.

Other

The purpose of this file is to keep records of all correspondence with other people you deal with on a general basis. This might include sections such as 'investor mentor' and 'my training'.

One section will include an overview of your 'Monthly Diary'. Although your letting agent should programme these events for you, it is advisable that you keep a record of this.

With this diary sheet to hand (for the whole year) you will always be able to keep on top of these activities and never miss a crucial moment. Don't forget to update it every time you do something and get into the habit of always checking it every two weeks. If a gas check is due for example, your letting agent will need to notify a Gas Safe Engineer a few weeks before.

The table below is a reminder of what is needed and when.

	Review	January	February	March
Property 1	Rent	Anytime		
	Tenancy	PERIODIC		
	EPC / PAT		2018 - Feb 18th	
	Gas			
	Inspection		DUE	
Property 2	Rent			6th
	Tenancy			6th
	EPC / PAT		28th PAT	
	Gas	14th		
	Inspection	DUE		
Property 3	Rent			12th
	Tenancy			12th
	EPC / PAT			
	Gas		24th	
	Inspection	DUE		

In this example, you will see:

- Property 1 is on Periodic tenancy, we can review the rent anytime (because it has been over a year since the last one), an inspection by us is due sometime in Feb; Gas and PAT checks are due later in the year and the next EPC is due in 2018 (10 years after the last one)

- Property 2 tenancy agreement is due 6th March at which time we will be reviewing the rent. Before we agree to a new tenancy, an inspection will be carried out; preferably just over 2 months prior to its expiration. Gas and PAT checks are due in January and February respectively.

Legal Compliance

I have already mentioned many of the legal requirements relating to buy-to-let properties. As a reminder, you will need to comply with:

- Tax Returns
- Insurance (contents, building and public liability)
- Assured Shorthold Tenancy Legislation
- Deposit Protection Legislation
- Health and Safety (Risk Assessment)
- Gas Safety
- Electrical Safety
- Fire Safety
- Energy Performance Certificate (EPC)
- Housing Health and Safety
- Mortgage Requirements
- Maintenance Contract (if any) Requirements
- Leaseholder Requirements (if applicable)

It is be best to seek further advice if you decide to undertake refurbishments, Houses in Multiple Occupation etc.

Legislation will change from time to time so you will need to keep up to date with the latest requirements.

Tax

You will need to complete a Tax self assessment when you start investing in property. You do not need an Accountant or Tax specialist to do this but you must take advice if this is new to you.

The specific part of the Tax Return you will need to complete is the "Land and Property" section for the annual profit and loss accounts. If you are selling an investment property you will need to complete the "Capital Gains" section.

In order to complete these efficiently and correctly you will need to have your 'property accounts' already prepared.

Managing Your Property Account

The best way to ensure that all of your property income and expenditure is recorded is to open a new and separate bank account. This does not need to be in a business name. Use this account to write cheques; make on-line payments; pay direct debits and standing orders; and collect all rental payments. You may also wish to set up a specific credit card account solely for making purchases to take advantage of any 'free' credit. Do not spend more than you have. It is essential that you check that your rent is being paid to you on time, every time.

Chapter 8 - Step 7: Reviewing the property value and refinancing

When I started investing in property, I thought that investing was simply 'buying houses that rented out'. I have since learned that is not the whole story.

This is how I became enlightened as to the final fundamental step of property investing.

My 2nd life changing moment

When we first remortgaged our own home, we really only had enough cash to buy two properties comfortably. We bought both of these in May 2002. The letting agent found tenants and everything was fine. With this in mind, we thought it would be a good idea to scrape up sufficient money for a deposit for a third house. We bought this in December 2002.

The following May, five months later, we were on the beach at Weston Super-Mare when Rachel told me that she was concerned about our finances. She suggested that we sell one of the houses!

This did not make sense to me because by now, I realized that the journey we had begun was the start of something fantastic. It was (potentially) a 10 year retirement plan. The income and the capital growth from the houses were going to give us financial independence. If we sold a house now, it was almost like saying our strategy wasn't working.

However, we realized that we had overstretched ourselves because we did not have any cash behind us to use. That is why we now recommend having a buffer account.

Anyway, I set off down the beach alone, to give myself time to think about this quietly. After about 30 minutes I worked it out. I returned to Rachel and said

"We are not going to sell a house. We are going to remortgage the first two and BUY two more!"

And I proceeded to tell Rachel how this would work.

We spoke to our financial advisor, and he agreed that my idea would work. So that's what we did. In September 2003 we bought our next two properties.

We had now learnt the full investment process – how to evaluate your assets and to work out if any capital can be released, so that your money works even harder for you. We also learnt that we needed a buffer account.

Putting into practice what we have learnt

Once I realised this final step, I now always consider what will happen to my investment in a year or two's time; rather than simply 'hoping' it will be ok. The long term strategy for creating financial freedom revolves around being able to refinance the property and take out all, or most of, your original investment. The quicker this can be done, the quicker financial freedom can happen.

The way to do this is to review all your investment property values, every 6 to 9 months, checking to see how much other similar properties in the same street or locality are selling at, or are on the market for.

If you bought the property for 15 to 25 percent below the surveyed value, and you bought it in a demand location, the property should now be valued at the original survey value plus a bit more.

You can do a simple calculation to see how much money you could now release. In fact, this is the hypothetical calculation that we do even before buying the property to satisfy ourselves that this will be possible / probable. So the result of your review should not come as any surprise – just confirmation.

Top Tip Think very carefully before you refinance the same property for a second time. A potential problem arises if you remortgage more than once, not least your ability to pay off Capital Gains when you come to sell the property.

Our first investment property purchase

We bought a house that needed a little work to make it suitable for renting out. This work was mainly painting and carpets.

At that time we also had the benefit from a rising property market.

You can see that we refinanced after just 18 months and this generated more money in our hands than we put into the property to start with.

Refinancing Calculations		
INITIAL COSTS (Feb 02)		
Purchase price		£76,000
Legal costs		£2,000
Add Value		£400
TOTAL COSTS		£78,400
FUNDED BY		
Mortgage	£60,000	
Own money	£18,400	
TOTAL USED	£78,400	
REFINANCING (Aug 03)		
New Property Value		£105,000
New Mortgage		£85,600
PAID BACK		
Original Mortgage	£60,000	
Money to start again	£25,600	
The money to start again of £25,600 is more than the original £18,400 we put into the property in the beginning. WOW		

You now know the 7 step process; and that you need to

buy the right property in the right location at the right price.

So what are you going to do now?

How determined are you to achieve financial independence?

PART IV

Knowing what you know - helping you start today

Many people fail to take action when they are presented with opportunities. Often they feel they do not have:

- Enough money
- Enough time
- Sufficient knowledge

 Or they are scared of changing; they have negative thoughts about the consequences of doing something different. 'It won't work for me though, will it?'

In this part, I hope to address these issues by explaining:

- Why you should start taking action today
- Money management – how to create your investment pot
- What next and other opportunities

TAKING targeted ACTION is the ONLY way to make changes – so START TODAY

· · · · ·

"You can't cross a sea by merely staring into the water."

Rabindranath Tagore was the first non-European to win the Nobel Prize in 1913 for his Literature, which was viewed as spiritual and mercurial.

· · · · ·

CHAPTER 9
Why start taking action today

My thoughts on our changing world

Pensions

The way most people were taught about pensions was informally; no structured learning. This means that we did not hear a consistent message. The result is that we don't really know what to do.

Employers are probably the first people that bring the concept of pensions to our attention. We find out that there is a state pension which you need to contribute to and when you reach Government-set retirement age, the Government will give you money each week.

We now know that the Government can no longer be

confident that it can provide sustainable pensions in the future. **So the amount of money we will get in retirement is unknown.**

Most large Government employers used to provide a pension that was directly related to your final salary. You could assess where you might be on the corporate ladder and its accompanying salary. This would give you a clue as to how much money your pension would give you when you reached retirement age.

However, the way in which these final salary schemes have been run in the past, means that these schemes are underfunded. The outcome is that these schemes are not being offered anymore: and many that are currently being paid out will have changed by the time you retire.

Nowadays, most Government employees and private company employees will get a pension based upon the contributions they make until they retire. These 'defined contribution' schemes do not guarantee the income they will generate in your retirement; it all depends upon how well your contributions are invested and the performance of those investments. **So the amount of money we will get in retirement is unknown.**

Financial Advisors offer advice. They suggest various companies and institutions where you should invest your money. If you opt for the 'low risk' option then your returns are likely to be limited; which possibly means a significant drop in your standard of living on retirement. For example, if you invest your money in a savings account in the bank, then you are lucky if your money keeps up with inflation. Would the £100 that you put in the bank today buy the same amount of goods that £102 would buy in a years' time? (The £102 is made up from £100 x bank savings interest rate of 2%)

 Even low to medium risk options still involve some degree of risk and the high risk option is exactly that. **Fundamentally, financial advisors are not in control of your investment, and neither are you.**

Pensions and Lifestyle

Even if I could predict the income that I would receive in retirement from these sources; would I be able to live the lifestyle I would like? Would I have to make sacrifices in order to survive? Would I need to sell my home to be able to make ends meet? Is anyone going to pay my medical bills when I am ill?

I spoke about this earlier in Chapter 2 and my conclusion was:

The Government is unlikely to be able to help us.

What this means to us:

- We cannot rely on the Government to fully support us in retirement

- Many pension schemes offered today do not give us any certainty as to our income in retirement

- We will need to keep contributing more and more to our pensions to ensure we get something reasonable back

- We need to gain control of our pension provision ourselves

Jobs are no longer for life

Very few jobs are for life. I believe the working world has changed and people, especially young people, should not expect a job for life. People either need to become highly skilled and keep acquiring more skills to enable them to adapt to the changing marketplace; or they need to build their own safety net and become less dependent on the salary generated by their working income. The world is becoming more entrepreneurial.

Now is the time to decide where you want to be and plan a way to get there

Make a plan and take action.

Wealthy people are visionaries and have a very strong desire to succeed. This means that they invest their time and money into reaching their desire, their goal. They do not allow themselves to be distracted from following their plan.

What is your WHY?

This is a reminder for you to remember "the Why" that you thought about at the beginning of the book.

Do not wait for an external kick start. Do not wait until you realize you need the extra cash. Do not wait until an unfortunate event befalls you. Create your life; starting today.

To change the way we think about money, we need a WHY. Why would you want more money? What would be its purpose? If your purpose is great enough and strong enough, it will give you passion to make it happen.

Once you have found your Why, you become committed to making that happen. Then anything is possible. Although I am talking about money specifically, it is not about the money. It is what money can do, that really counts.

• • • • •

The bigger the "Why" the easier the "How"

Jim Rohn

• • • • •

What is your ideal world going to look like?

Just pause for a moment and jot down what makes you happy now.

There are many ways people lead fulfilling lives. Some thoughts are:

- Family and Friends
- Romance
- Spiritual
- Community
- Health

- Finances
- Fun and Recreation
- Personal Growth
- Physical Environment
- Career and Business

• • • • •

"If you can dream it, you can do it"

Walt Disney (1901 – 1966)

• • • • •

EXERCISE

What would make your future just perfect, in say 10 years time? Be as specific as you can.

If money was no object because you have £20m in the bank; maybe using the ideas above; what would make your future absolutely perfect?

Make your dreams **BIG**

Some people create 'vision boards' from pictures, photos, texts etc that depict the life and lifestyle they want to achieve. Many people understand this as their 'bucket list' – a list of things they would like to achieve before they die.

These life goals should become *YOUR NEW NEEDS*. Focus on them. Sit back and close your eyes for a moment. What do you hear? What do you smell? How do you think you will *FEEL* when you have achieved these things?

Use these dreams to start making a plan. What is it you want to achieve or do? How much money is needed? Will your income, investments and pension provide you with enough?

You need to focus on ways to bring about the money needed to fund them. Your current income must now expand to allow you to fulfil your new needs.

You are now in a position to start making those goals a reality by setting some specific targets, plans and ACTIONS.

Setting your goals

Do you know what your goals are now? What your vision is?

Without goals you cannot plan a way to get there. You tend to drift along, fighting from one day to another to make ends meet. You have no clear direction.

One of my roles as a Chartered Civil Engineer was to arrange for 'things to be done on time and to budget'. This could be design work, inspections, repair work, building work etc. I developed systems of work to ensure I minimised the risk of missing any of my time deadlines, quality requirements and monetary budgets. In order to do this I needed to analyse the task in hand, work out what needed to be done, by when and by whom. From this I could set a host of targets – which could be monitored to ensure compliance. I helped other managers set targets and measures for their work; and over time I became known as the 'Performance Manager'.

In my role as Performance Manager, I was able to help individuals and organizations set measureable goals and realistic performance targets. The problem I found was that managers try to set goals and targets that 'stretched' their staff and organizations too far. The targets were never going to be achieved and so no-one bothered to try.

My skill was setting targets, which were important to achieve, in order to deliver improvements. They also had to be realistic, so that everyone could actually see how it could work, if undertaken correctly.

Weight loss example

Recently I decided I would love to lose one and half stone in weight but I hated exercise and I loved my food.

So the method of losing weight could not involve just eating less or doing exercise. If it did, I would not be able to keep that up – I would fail.

After talking to various friends, I decided I would eat different and healthier foods that would not be so fattening. My target therefore was to eat healthy foods and cut out bread.

Within 5 months I had lost 2 stone. I succeeded because the plan I chose to implement was in my control; and was achievable and realistic.

The reason I mention this is because you need to know what constitutes 'a success'; otherwise, how will you *know when you are successful and when you can be happy;* and therefore be able to celebrate your successes?

Once you have a clear SMART target (Specific, Measurable, Achievable, Realistic and Time bound) then you can start to check your progress. You can do this for any aspect of your life. But you do need to set them now, for your financial future. When you begin to measure and check, then your mind becomes focused and that helps you even more to get past that winning post.

I have met some people that are unsure whether they can actually achieve anything at all. If you are one of these people, then I understand that it is not easy to set SMART targets because you may not have an expectancy of achieving anything. If you are like this, then maybe this next idea might help.

Firstly, picture in your mind where you would really love to be in few years time. Just choose one happy thought – that maybe you could say, "wouldn't it be wonderful to be ... to do ..." **Do not worry about how or if** you can actually get there. Now just think of one, maybe two, VERY small steps that might help you move towards your happy thought.

Stemming from the concept of 'eating an elephant', once you have your big dreams and big targets, break them down into bite-sized chunks. Make these chunks the focus of your attention and the immediate call on your time and resources. As you gradually work through the chunks, your big goal will become closer.

Climbing Snowdon, the highest mountain in Wales – in little chunks

My Dad decided he wanted to climb Snowdon for his 80th Birthday. My son and I agreed to help him. He did not want to take the train up. He wanted to walk.

Just after the Half-Way House, the climb gets very steep and by now my Dad was not in very good shape. He insisted that we carry on. After an hour's rest prior to this section, my son and I agreed to help Dad make further progress. However I don't think any of us had an expectation of reaching the top.

We did agree a rule though; that we would not think about getting to the top. We would only set the next target, which was a particular rock just 5 metres higher. At each rock we got to, we rested and then set out for the next rock, again only 5 metres higher.

Eventually we made it to the top of this steep section around 250 metres higher. We continued to the top – and my Dad was extremely happy and worn out.

He did not even want to take the train down – it was a great accomplishment.

Do you have to see your complete journey to know you are going to get to your destination?

Car journey at night

This is a little like taking a car journey at night. You started on this particular road because the direction signs told you that this is the way to ... "wonderland". Because it is dark, you cannot see the whole of the route set out before you. You can only see the short distance where your lights shine.

However, you have an expectation, due to your previous experience, that the road will continue and that it will take you to your intended destination.

When you begin to follow the road that successful people have journeyed, aren't you likely to end up where they ended up? You can attain your dreams by setting a course of action that others have experienced before you: by following their signposts; their actions.

Once you start on this journey, I am sure you will begin to feel inspired, liberated and in control of your finances. You will feel wonderful when you get there!

Setting targets to succeed

You can decide how to measure whether you are successful or not. Do not set targets and actions that you cannot control.

Examples of things not (completely) within your control: are winning the lottery, being healthy, relying on handouts, and having a well paid job.

What is in your control: investing in assets, eating healthily, being happy, taking control of your finances, pleasing your employers.

Do not hope the elements or other people will be on your side.

EXERCISE

Write down around eight bite-sized specific targets that will help you attain your 'perfect future'.

For example: if you wish to help a particular charity; your bite-sized targets maybe along the lines of:

- I will volunteer 1 hour of my time each week
- I will organise a fundraising coffee morning every 2 months
- I will arrange a social fundraising event once a year

 If you would like help in developing this further for yourself and / or your family, come along to one of my workshops. See my website www.mylifesolutions.co.uk for details

The journey to Retire Early Retire Wealthy also requires you to gain control of your money

CHAPTER 10
Money management

I have noticed that most people spend all the money they earn and some spend even more. Our personality profile, our upbringing and our lack of education in money management has a great deal to do with this behaviour, spending all we get. In addition, even those people that do save, still spend their savings on liabilities rather than assets.

By providing you with the education that will help you to create a pot of money, you can start investing in assets today.

The problem with spending all your income is that you will not be able to gain control of your life, for the whole of your life. At some stage, your income is going to change and you will need to find another form of income to replace it, like a pension. Otherwise you will have to change your lifestyle to suit your new lower income boundaries.

I believe money is important because it makes life more enjoyable. Not just for the person with the money, but for all those people around them.

To me it's not about the money, it's what money can bring, not just for you but for others. Maybe you want to support a charity: you can't do that if you cannot free up some time or some money. So, although I am concentrating on 'money', my underlying reason for creating money is to make good use of it for me, my family and for the benefit of everyone that comes into my world. I want to add value to other people's lives.

Money allows us to do things that are good to do, as well as pay for the essentials of life. I was going to say 'necessities' but maybe doing something that makes us feel good is actually a necessity as well. Paying for things that make us feel good not only makes us happy, but also helps the money to flow. Someone else gets your payment and this makes them happy. They can now go off and use this income. Money likes to flow.

The reason for introducing money management to you is that I have come to realize there is more to this than simply managing your expenses within your income. I did this at home and I even did this as part of my day job when I used to look after multi-million pound budgets. But this is not the whole story.

Why is it that many of the winners of big prizes, soon lose all the money that they won? They did not understand money management. I believe this also applies to many other people.

I encourage you to play the money game to win. This does not mean gamble or contrive. This simply means gaining control of your finances so the rest of your life can follow. Money management is a technique that works for everyone if you are prepared to put a little effort into it. This may mean you will have to make some changes to the way you look after your money at the moment; but in the end you will come to realize what a fantastic difference it makes. You will be able to employ this technique for the remainder of your life, even when you have a lot of money. I would go as far to say, especially when you have a lot of money, or a large income. The money could soon be gone if not used wisely.

Gaining control of your finances

Gaining control of your finances is vitally important if you desire a secure future for you and your loved ones. Gaining control will help you do the things that are maybe only dreams at the moment.

My goal is to help you become financially independent.

The exercises in this chapter will help you to manage your finances so you can create a pot of money. This money should only be used to help you become financially free. It should not be used for anything else.

The exercises we are going to do are designed to:

- Identify your income and expenditure needs
- Identify ways where you can save a little
- Show you additional income opportunities
- Show you how the money management system helps create your investment pot

Good debt versus bad debt

I believe our financial world is changing and we should not rely on credit to pay for things that we cannot really afford. We should only use good debt.

Top Tip The ONLY time you should use other people's money, i.e. a loan or credit, is when you have a sure way to pay off the interest and repay the capital borrowed.

If you use the borrowed money to buy an asset then this is considered "good debt". An asset is something that will put money in your pocket, i.e. you get more in than you pay out: on interest etc.

If you use the borrowed money to pay for something that does not put money in your pocket, and you are borrowing the money because you cannot really afford the item at the moment, then this is "bad debt".

Where are you now?

I have created a few exercises for you to do. You will benefit if you collate the information as you go, even if it is approximate to start with. However, you will only get the real benefit if you introduce this learning into your life for real – not just have it at the back of your mind.

Templates to help complete these exercises can be found on my website.

This chapter only concerns your CURRENT income and expenses.

For the following exercises, I find it best to convert *regular* income and expenses to 'monthly' figures; and allocate **intermittent** income and expenses to the month in which they are due.

Don't spend more money than you earn.

This requires you to know several things:

1. How much money you get in

2. How much do you actually spend

3. How much do you really need to spend

Income

Most people will know fairly well what their current income is. This is derived from one or several sources. Some examples are:

- Salary
- Investment income
- Pensions
- Government Benefits
- Gifts
- Inheritance
- Dividends from a company

These come to you in the form of:

- regular known incomes

- regular unknown incomes
- annual known incomes
- annual unknown incomes
- intermittent incomes

EXERCISE

Know your income

Using the appropriate income streams listed above, and any others of your own, record your income as a monthly amount. You can do this as an individual person even if you are sharing a home because you will know your share of the expenses. Alternatively you can combine incomes with a partner, husband or wife if you share all expenses. Do this exercise in whichever way is best for your circumstances.

Income stream	January	February	March
Job 1 basic			
Job 1 overtime / bonus			
Job 2			
Child Benefit			
Child Tax Credit			
pension 1			
pension 2			
pension 3			
Total			

How much do you actually spend?

You may know this as 'all of it'. Well, that's not really good enough. We need to analyse this a little deeper.

Maybe a better question I should ask is

"What things do you spend your money on AND how much do you actually spend on each of those things?"

The next exercise will help you with this.

EXERCISE

Record your regular expenses

Using this table as a guide, record the items that you spend your money on and how much.

Expenditure - regular	January	February	March
Council Tax			
Gas			
Electric			
Water			
TV			
Broadband			
Phone			
Petrol			
Clothes			
Health Care			
Entertainment			
Food			
Pet			
Total			

EXERCISE

Record your non-regular expenses

Some of the other expenditure items that people often spend on a non-regular basis are shown below.

Adding your own items, record the items that you spend your money on and how much. This exercise is for your non-regular expenses

It is important to identify the month in which you pay out your money on these expenses.

Expenditure non-regular	January	February	March
Holidays			
Household insurance			
Car repairs			
Replace household goods			
Presents / Gifts			
Hobbies			
Total			

Top Tip If you find a lot of expenses in one or two particular months, then work out a way to move some of them to a different month. Maybe even convert a large single item to a monthly spend – such as house insurance maybe. Or start putting money aside for items like 'Christmas', earlier in the year.

The idea is to have a consistent monthly spend if at all possible.

Analysis of income and expenditure

Now take a look at your income and expenditure totals. Do the numbers appear to reflect your understanding of them? Do they match reality? For example, if these number show that you have more money at the end of the month, than you normally do, then something is not quite right.

When you go through these exercises, you will probably come to a point where you have accounted for most of your income. You might not be sure about the rest of the expenditure though. What many people forget about is the items of expenditure that occur later in the year, like the car MOT, the house insurance, your friend's birthday. People tend to underestimate the effect of not making a provision for these so it is important to identify them and take them into account in your budget; otherwise you will not have enough money to pay for them. Or do you spend too much physical cash without really knowing what it is spent on?

We tend to spend the money we have and if we don't have a bill to pay in the month, we may be tempted to use that money in another way.

Top Tip

- Ensure that you fully understand your income and expenditure.
- Allocate your cash as best you can to expenditure categories.
- Check your cash and bank accounts regularly, at least weekly.

I think the reason for our desire to spend all that we earn comes down to either:

- We cannot afford the most basic essentials in life: this is not entirely our fault
- We have no reason NOT to spend it.

I know that some people do save for things they want, such as holidays, cars, and a deposit for a home.

Later in life, some become aware that their pension provision will not be adequate for their future needs. So they start to save, or accept that they will downsize their current home or way of living to suit their future income.

Before we go on, you should remember that I want to help you to look for ways to collect a pot of money together, so that you can start investing in your future and you will not have to rely on somebody else in later years.

How much do you really need to spend?

I think the best way I can introduce you to understanding how much you really need to spend is for you to consider the things you COULD cut out if you suddenly found you needed to save some money for something.

This is different for everyone.

If you have a large income, your need to spend money will be different than if you don't have a lot of money. Let me explain.

If you don't have much money, a treat for you or your family might be to go to an expensive restaurant once in a while. Even 'expensive' is a relative term and relates to your current lifestyle.

This is also different for everyone.

If you have a reasonable income, then a trip to the expensive restaurant could be the place where you meet new clients and where your clients expect you to be. This becomes essential for you rather than a treat.

The good thing about the money management technique is that it works for everyone. It is essential for everyone; whether you have money or not. The next few exercises will help you clarify your thoughts on 'how much do I really need to spend'.

Creating an investment pot

 Earlier in the book I suggested that you should start putting away 10% of your income into your investment pot.

The idea here is that the first person you pay is YOURSELF. Get into this habit.

There are two ways to create your investment pot:

- Cut out some of your expenditure
- Increase your income

Cut some expenditure

You need to identify what parts of your expenditure you could reduce or cut out altogether. You might consider:

- Items I could reasonably easily cut out if I found a better way to use my money
- Items I could cut out with difficulty

EXERCISE

Expenditure items I could cut out if I needed to

Make a list of items you could cut back on together with the cash amount you could save. This should not be undertaken lightly, we are talking about the rest of your life here. If you already have savings or if you already contribute to a savings plan, that's great. But I suggest you still do this exercise because it will help you to form a new habit. Do both the following exercises.

Items I could reasonably easily cut out if, for example: my washing machine is broken and I need £500 to buy a new one. These are the items I will cut out for a few months. List them.

Items I could cut out with difficulty if, for example: my car needs £1500 to get it back on the road and I need my car for work. These are the items I will cut out for a few months. List them

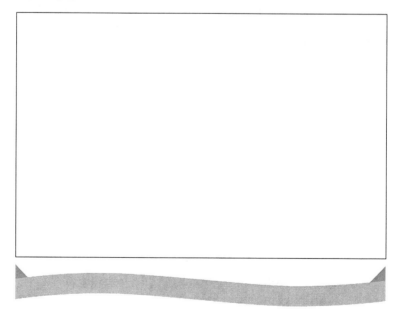

Now you have some potential areas where you can save some money if you really need to. I say 'need to' only because I have found that people do not take 'want to' seriously enough, to make them alter the way they behave. For many people, the main reason they change a habit is through fear of the present situation rather than a desire to achieve something different. Don't wait for that kick-start: it might be too late; start changing your habits today.

Cutting expenditure can only achieve so much though. There is a limit on the amount you can cut back depending upon your income and lifestyle. You will only make significant gains if you can also increase your income.

Increase your income

By finding 5 to 10 hours per week you could begin to create some extra income; and often very little start-up money is needed.

You may have already considered various ways to increase your income but let me share a few ideas that you might not have thought of:

- Network marketing
  - promoting products to your friends that you like or get benefit from
  - promoting them to other people's friends and colleagues
- On-line
  - Ebay - Buying products you know well – and selling them for more
  - Affiliate marketing – find products and services that are offered by other people; become an affiliate; promote them and get paid a commission.

- Create a product from your own experience. Everyone has a story to tell or a particular skill they have based upon work or a hobby. The product could be on-line teaching or regular classes that you give.

- Rent out your spare garage or car space if you live in an area where other people need parking

- Rent a room out – you may qualify for tax exemption on your profit

- Do ironing or something similar for others – this can be done in your own time at your convenience – whilst watching your favourite television programme.

- If you are a business owner, double your fees. If you lose only 40% of your customers you are still winning and you gain some time as well. You will need to do your analysis but the idea is to think big.

- If you are a business owner, look to offer your current clients another product rather than chase additional clients. If people are already buying from you, then I am sure they will buy the add-on. Remember the add-on may not even be your product. Link with a colleague to joint venture and make it a win-win for everyone.

Go to my website for more ideas

If you feel that your product or service would fit or compliment the products already shown on my website, then I would be delighted to consider starting a joint venture with you; even if you are just 'thinking about starting' at this stage. Let me know through the contact-us page on my website www.mylifesolutions.co.uk

An idea -

If you begin to increase your income by just 1% in the first month in a sustainable way, and do the same in month 2 and so on, this turns into a whopping 12% increase by the end of one year.

Example: You would like to earn an additional £200 per month

You could find a company you like and recommend it to a friend. For this, you could get a commission of £25. If you do this once per week, you will earn £100 per month.

After one year you will have 50 customers. If you are paid an ongoing commission of around £2 per month for each customer, this means after a year you also get a passive income (an income where you do not have to do any extra work) of £100 per month.

After one year you are now generating £200 per month additional income. Many people take this sort of business – Network Marketing - very seriously and reap huge benefits.

 If you like this idea, you may find a company on my website that you could promote.

How much extra income do you need?

What is your big dream and how much money will you need to accomplish it? I recommend that you think big at this stage. There is no harm in thinking big and there will be a fair chance of being successful. My BIG DREAMS are:

My BIG Dream	Likely cost
Total	

Now you can start thinking about how you might earn that sort of income. What skills do you have that you could use. How many people could you help with your knowledge or product? How could you start helping them?

The more you start exercising your mind in this way, the more likely it is that you will sub-consciously see opportunities.

This next exercise is designed to help you build up your investment pot – so that you can buy assets that will help create your wealth, so that you can attain your dreams. Take it seriously – it is your desired life you are aiming to create today.

EXERCISE

Generate £5,000 over a short period of time

My partner needs an operation next year to help him walk better. It's going to cost £5,000. This is what I am going to do over the next few months to save or earn that money.

Ways I will reduce my expenditure	Amount £

Ways I will increase my income	Amount £

To take this one stage further, ask yourself *how you would increase your income substantially* if you really needed to.

As you do this next exercise you should clear your mind of everything else AND take it seriously. It will be hard; but you will come up with ideas; you then need to delve deeper into each one to find clarity. Take your time and be as specific as you can.

I know this sounds a bit dramatic, but it's a really useful way of helping to prioritise your actions if *you REALLY want to change your future.*

EXERCISE

Generate £50,000 over a short period of time

My daughter needs an operation next year that will save her life. It's going to cost £50,000. This is what I am going to do over the next few months to get that money. Use any ideas, including those already generated from this book.

Ways I will reduce my expenditure	Amount £

Ways I will increase my income	Amount £

Now you have got a few ideas to work on. They may seem a bit daunting so 'chunk' these down into manageable bits, as described in the previous chapter.

When you get to the end of the exercises you can prioritise your list to suit your particular circumstances.

You can do it

Some people may say "I haven't got enough time" or "I haven't got enough money". These are just excuses that can be overcome.

If it is "time" you are worried about, go through the exercise I set earlier about cutting expenses. Do the same for "time". I have found many people spend lots of time watching television. Maybe this is a place to start. You only need to find around 5 hours a week to make a difference to your future.

We all have different periods of the day or week when we are at our most creative or productive. Some people get a 'second wind' in the evening. To avoid breaking into your 'creative' time, record programmes that you really want to watch. Use the 'creative' time to start generating ideas and ultimately an additional income stream. Give up a little now and in 10 to 15 years time, you will have as much time as you want to do whatever you like.

Some ideas, like ironing and home packaging, can be done in front of the TV. You may be surprised by children's eagerness to help: they see it as fun!

All of the ideas I gave earlier are low cost entry ideas. But if it's start-up money you are still concerned about, maybe you could consider a joint venture. Think of someone that believes in you and your idea and borrow some money from them, or give them a percentage of the profit.

You now have several ways to increase your income and have an idea of how much that could be.

The technique I am going to share with you next will help you to keep control of your finances.

Your personality profile affects your money habits

This money management system is ideal for all personalities. Olivia Mellan states, in her book 'Money Harmony', that there are four main money profiles:

- Spenders
- Savers
- Avoiders - Hide their head in the sand because they don't want to deal with money
- Monks - Believe money is beneath them and don't care about material things

With a little coaching and a clear direction, I believe all these personality types will benefit because the system is going to allow:

- 'Spenders' to spend – up to a limit – and promote saving as well
- 'Savers' to save – but will promote spending by having fun - up to a limit
- 'Avoiders' to take control of their finances
- 'Monks' to promote order with their finances to allow money to flow better

And most of all, everyone will be able to create an investment pot.

The money pot management system

Money management is quite a simple concept and was fashionable for my grandparents. I said earlier that we need to forget using credit. During my grandparent's time, the only acceptable credit available was at the pawn shop. Even then you had to leave an item of value before the lender would give you credit against it.

My grandparents were given their wages in cash. From this cash they had to set aside money to pay for their rent; electric; gas; food; new or second-hand shoes etc; or save up for their daughter's wedding. They used to have tin-pots for each of item of expenditure. When they got paid, their cash was divided out into these pots. If there was anything left, they could treat themselves. Some people might have saved a little as well.

So the categories of expenditure that come from this story are:

- Accommodation
- Utilities
- Food and other household essentials
- Short term savings (for things later in the year)
- Long term savings (for things in later years)
- Non-essentials (treats to spend on themselves)
- Savings (for a rainy day)

For some of us, this is our budget-planning process as well: myself included, up until a couple of years ago.

What takes this to a new level, however, is adding in a couple more categories. I said this was simple when you think about it – but not many of us do. It was T. Harv Eker that introduced this concept to me and I am truly grateful. It seems to have brought several themes together that I treated in a disjointed way.

The additional items are:

- Giving
- Education
- Investment pot

 The idea here is that you create new pots for charity, improving your own knowledge base and investing for your future.

Make a specific pot for them rather than just hoping you get around to making these things happen.

The bit I love is the title 'investment pot' rather than savings. This gives the pot so much more meaning; it makes me think about creating my future rather than some 'just in case' pot that can be dipped into whenever I find a suitable reason to use it.

There is a rule relating to the 'investment pot' and that is you must "only use this money to invest in assets"; never spend it on anything else.

The Education pot also allows us to invest some money on our learning which will, in turn, help us to succeed better along any particular path we want to travel. This could be learning a hobby, learning a new skill or taking an educational programme. So now, if you thought selling on-line or property investing was a good idea, you will have a way to pay for your training to learn to do it successfully rather than 'dipping-in' and hoping.

There is one more item I need to add here. If you currently have credit cards, or similar, where you are paying interest on the balance, you need to pay these off quickly. This is eating into the money available to use for other things. You could be paying over 20% per year on this money so clearing the bad debt quickly is paramount. You need to create a pot specifically for paying off credit cards and bad debt.

You need to cut out some of your expenditure you identified in the earlier exercise "items I could cut out". The quicker you pay these high interest repayments off, the sooner you will have more money in your pocket.

 But remember pay into your investment pot first. This will help you create a new habit.

If we rename the original list, we have our NEW expenditure pots as follows:

- Essentials (to include all items we consider essential like accommodation, utilities, food, petrol, etc)
- Short-term savings
- Long-term savings (and you may have several of these)
- Giving
- Education

- Investment pot
- Clear bad debt
- Fun

Where did the 'Fun' pot come from?

The 'fun money' is the money you can spend on yourself. In fact the rule is that you *MUST spend it each month*. Treat yourself to whatever takes your fancy: like a round of golf, eating out, a pamper weekend: or put it aside for a couple of months and take a short holiday break.

It is specifically designed to allow 'Savers' to spend without feeling bad about it! 'Spenders' probably use too much 'fun' money already and need to cut back and put it to other uses.

If your children start moaning about 'not having the latest ...whatever': then why not begin teaching them the importance of money management and how they can begin?

How the money management system works

The money management system works by putting a percentage of your income into various pots. You may need to adjust some of the percentages to suit your situation, but the principle must be adhered to, so that you get the best chance of ALWAYS managing your money, no matter what your particular circumstances are. The order of allocation is essential. Don't forget to 'keep a little of what you earn' – in your investment pot.

In the following table, I suggest targets to aim for. These will be achievable over time but I recognise that this will be a difficult starting position for most people.

Identify your money pot starting position

Gather your actual income and expenditure from the earlier exercises. Combine the expenses into the pots listed below and record exactly how much you spend against each one. You can then convert them to percentages to see where you are starting from.

Action	TARGET		Your Starting Position	
	% allocation	Example of Value £	Your starting %	Your £ income and expenses
Identify your net income per month		2000		
Your expenses:				
Investment Pot	10%	£200		
Clear bad debt	zero	zero	See note 'bad debt; below	
Essentials	55%	£1,100		
Fun	10%	£200		
Short-term savings	5%	£100		
Long-term savings	5%	£100		
Education	10%	£200		
Giving	5%	£100		

I have put 'Giving' last, only on the basis that you will be able to help more later on when you have more. It's a bit like a lioness looking after her young cubs. She has to feed herself first so that she is strong and has the best chance of finding food again. The cub is only fed when the mother has had sufficient to keep her fit and ready to 'go again'. You could even combine giving with having fun, like organising a sponsored walk or a charity meal with a few friends.

 Using the ideas you have generated for cutting expenditure and increasing your income, you may wish to set interim targets for yourself which could be achieved in the next THREE months.

Note – bad debt You need to clear this as quickly as possible. You need to rethink what you are spending your money on. Use this money management system as quickly as possible. Choose an amount you are going to commit to paying off the bad debt. Let us say, this is £200 per month.

Create your own money pot allocation in order to clear bad debts

Your pots may look like this example. Create your own allocation.

	Interim TARGET		Your Starting Position	
Action	Maybe start % allocation	Example of Value £	YOUR target %	Your target amount £
Identify your net income per month		2000		
Your expenses:				
Investment Pot	2%	£40		
Clear bad debt	10%	200		
Essentials	75%	£1,500		
Fun	3%	£60		
Short-term savings	3%	£60		
Long-term savings	3%	£60		
Education	3%	£60		
Giving	1%	£20		

So the rules are:

1. Allocate money to your Investment Pot first. Create a new habit.

2. Clear bad debt and credit cards where you are paying interest

3. Identify how much you can allocate to Fun for spending on treats. Spend all of this every month. Or maybe combine a couple of months to spend on some bigger treat.

4. Identify what you need in the coming months, maybe a holiday or a new fridge and try and allocate sufficient money into your savings pots. Combine short-term and long-term to suit your needs. You probably spend money on these anyway. You are simply allocating a specific pot to them now.

5. Have a look at your normal spending habits and identify what you really need to spend money on. Allocate a suitable amount to Essentials. If you normally spend more, is there another pot you should be creating?

6. Education should be given priority over Giving at this stage. The reason is that the more you learn the more you will be able to earn, especially if you target learning skills related to the creation of additional, preferably passive, income streams.

10. THE MOST IMPORTANT RULE IS THAT YOU NEVER SPEND your Investment Pot money. This is only to be invested in assets.

Top Tip Put away 10% of your income every month.

It may be difficult at first but you will get used to it.

Maybe start in month 1 by

- cutting expenditure by 1%
- finding 1% extra income

Try and drive a wedge between your income and expenditure

Repeat each month until you are able to put 10% a month away

Use the remaining 90% to live off.

NEVER SPEND YOUR INVESTMENT POT

If invested wisely, it will eventually provide you with a passive income, more than the amount you need to live your desired life. Then, and only then, can you start to spend the generated income if you choose to.

Summary

I hope that you now understand why playing the money game to win is important. You should know where you spend your money and how you want to use it in the future, *Starting Today*.

Go on, create an Investment Pot and invest this money in assets. Only purchase items that put money into your pocket and not take it out.

If you are starting a business, ensure you systemise it, so that the income will be generated without too much of your time.

And don't forget to use your Fun money to enjoy yourself every month.

I hope that this book helps you realize that the road you are about to embark upon is no longer a dream!

YOU can create your future

CHAPTER 11
What next and other opportunities

I know this can be a daunting moment. "I have found an opportunity; I think it would work: I wonder if it would work for me?", "am I too late to do this?", "how do I really get started?" "I don't know enough to be sure that I can make it work".

Frequent comments I hear

Many people say to me "I wish I had done what you have done. It is too late for me now though. I've missed the boat."

Or, "you are lucky to be able to stop work. You have been lucky. I wish I could have done that."

Well, the facts are: what we have achieved has not been down to luck; and also, you cannot go back in time. However, by recognising today that there is a better way forward, you can begin to consider 'when is the best time to start my journey?'

I have shown you, using the graphs earlier, that property prices have, in the past, doubled every 7 to 10 years. So whenever you start to invest in property, you know that your property will increase in value over time. I have also shown you techniques that professional investors use to increase the value of property even faster than this.

A word of warning: many people seem to take on their friends' advice and agree with them even though they are not experts. The trouble with property is that everyone is an expert because everyone lives in a property of some sort. They all have experiences to share: real or imagined; based on hearsay or articles. I hope you realize from reading *Retire Early Retire Wealthy* that investing in property for cash flow and long term wealth creation is a serious profession. To excel, you need to treat it as such and not a hobby. Talk to, and learn from, a professional property advisor.

The 'what if up game'

Why not play the 'what if up' game? This is when you consider the upside of a situation or opportunity. Many people don't realize it but they play the 'what if down' game. They always find reasons why the situation or opportunity will not work; especially for them. And of course their friends agree!

• • • • •

"Whether you think you can or you can't – either way you are right"

Henry Ford (July 30, 1863 – April 7, 1947) was an American industrialist, the founder of the Ford Motor Company and a pioneer of 'welfare capitalism'.

• • • • •

So I am suggesting that you ask yourself "what if this really works?" Wouldn't that be great? Wouldn't that be fantastic?

What I would like to say to you is that, when you begin to invest in property, you can expect to feel...

- Inspired
- Liberated
- In control of your finances
- In control of your life

Now, you may say that you enjoy your current job, or running your own business. Your life is great the way it is; that's brilliant. But do you see the significant benefits that investing in UK property can bring? It will enable you to have choices about the way you lead your life in the future: maybe 10, maybe 15 years time. Keep your job; enjoy your job even more, knowing that you and not your employer, are in control of your life.

During the last few years, meeting with other property investors, it is so refreshing to see that everyone enjoys working with others in the industry. We create win-win joint ventures. We share information and always give our clients the best service we can. In a recent 'large refurbishment' project that I did with a partner, he had the skills and the workforce; I had the spreadsheets, the planning and the marketing knowledge. We both shared the capital cost. We helped each other to make a good return on our investment.

I am working with investors that are turning large houses into self-contained units. My colleagues can offer a variety of property opportunities to suit your specific requirements; extremely good high growth properties or extremely good cash flow ones, for example. We share different models so that we can help each other and other people, like you, start your journey to financial freedom.

I have detailed knowledge of the buy-to-let market in various parts of the UK, and when my clients wish to invest in other parts of the country, my trusted colleagues will help find that ideal property for them. This applies to all the various investment strategies, including taking control of a house for a £1! How does that sound?

Property investors, who have been in this business for many years, know that the best way to do business is to work together. Partnering, or joint venturing (JV) with others, can save you years of learning and a lot of money: provided you find the right person to JV with. When left alone, most people will not take action.

For you, this means that you can choose to invest in property in a passive way if you want. You can find a company or individual that you like and trust, one that you feel you can do business with. You can work with them – to identify your requirements and jointly produce a plan that will start you on your journey. As new investment strategies arise, a mentor, like me, will keep you informed and make recommendations. With the 'passive' option, you will be able to go about your life knowing that you have taken care of your finances and long term wealth.

Should you wish to be more hands-on and take an active part in property investment, then there are brilliant trainers that can show you, how to find *the right property in the right location at the right price.*

The idea here is to form a friendship or a partnership with someone, or some company that you know you can trust. Once again, please be careful with whom you work. Do their work ethics align with yours? Are they primarily in business to look after themselves or to help their customers?

Top Tip The truth is that we will never achieve our full potential on our own. Daniel Priestley says that's why every great sports person has a coach; that's why a president has advisors; and why great actors have a director: always to bring out the best in them. Everyone needs a coach to get the best out of them.

Knowing the fundamentals

I encourage you to learn the fundamentals so that you can evaluate property options and opportunities yourself. Knowing the fundamentals is a must; otherwise you will be relying on someone else to make choices for you. I know from experience that not all people give good advice. People who have done this successfully before - like me - are willing to help you, be your mentor and help you make wise decisions.

To help you through this, I have designed various tools and educational programmes where I teach you how to invest in property, in a way which minimises risk. Once you have a grasp of the fundamentals, then you are in a position to take control yourself – and not get tempted by the latest 'special offer' that teaches you the latest fad on how to acquire property cheaply, for example.

Also, I have heard many stories and have experienced myself, that some training goes over the heads of many attendees. Either this: or the training is designed to give the attendee another full time job; or the specific strategy being learnt does not work in the trainee's area; or the trainee does not have the personal skills necessary to make it work for them.

The principles of my property education programme

Understanding the fundamentals is absolutely essential BEFORE you buy your investment property.

I have seen portfolios of so called 'property investors' that do not work. They failed to take account of the fundamentals. They did not make all the checks they should have done.

You have already begun to learn the fundamentals of property investing, including some of the checks that you need to do and some of the techniques to employ. You must know these whether you will be building up your property investment yourself, or working with someone else.

Top Tip You need to be in control of your property purchases. It is worth noting that over 95% of the 'good' purchases I am offered do not comply with my criteria.

In my education programme, I teach how to ensure that you *buy the right property in the right location at the right price,* in more detail and at a pace to suit you. Many investors do not know this – or get blinded by 'the great deal' and become potentially at risk. So spending time on the fundamental details is vitally important and this forms the basis of my property education programmes. In my community, we help each other with interesting aspects of money management and business development, as well as in-depth property investment. Would you like to join us?

We look at real purchase opportunities and use Roly's Property Analyser to test if they meet our criteria. If they do ... would you buy? Well, that would be up to you. I would suggest that this is unlikely at this stage, because we have not explored what YOU want. If you decide investing in UK property is for you, then we would go through your needs and help build up a plan just for you.

Everyone is different. Will you want high cash flow or great growth to create wealth? Or a mixture of both? What part of the country would you prefer to buy in? Will you want to manage the property yourself? How quickly do you want outcomes to happen? What is your 'investment risk' profile? This will influence both the type of purchase you should make and the methods of purchase that are best for you. Everyone is different and has a different need.

You will be able to arrange for property purchase opportunities to be sent to you. You can then do the numbers using Roly's Property Analyser. If any stack up, then you can consider buying them. You can arrange for someone else to find a tenant and manage the tenant and the property. I use a letting agent that operates nationwide. So you will be able to invest from the comfort of your own armchair.

When you know the fundamentals, this knowledge will last forever. You can make informed purchases for years to come, *but only* when you have mastered the fundamentals.

What you can expect from working with us

We are a family team with national support from numerous active property investors, trainers and advisors. This means you get far more than just our support. You are able to leverage our network of colleagues. We are not affiliated with any single company which means you will be offered help, if needed, only from the ones that are suited to provide the very best for your specific requirements.

We will respect you as a person and will treat you as we would expect to be treated ourselves. We will always be looking for a win-win between us. We will provide as much or as little help as you need.

We will hold you accountable if you need this 'to get stuff done'.

Our success depends totally on you being able to have the choice to **live the life you desire.** We genuinely want you to succeed as we have done ourselves. For so long, people have been told to get a good education; get a good job; work hard and save regularly for a decent pension. This does not work anymore. Let us help you and your children to have the mindset of the wealthy people.

You will view your job or your work in a different way. It will be much more pleasurable. You will not have to worry about getting promotion, or look for another job simply to get a higher salary. You will be much happier knowing that you are gaining control of your own finances ... so the rest of your life can follow.

You will have more time to yourself in a few years.

You can *Retire Early Retire Wealthy.*

Your next step

You have enough basic information in this book to start investing in property yourself, but it is wise to work with other people, to use the power of leverage by using their experience, skills and resources.

Investing in UK property is not a get rich fast scheme, but it is a well proven method of achieving wealth over a medium period of time - if done correctly.

I hope that by now you have come to the view that you want to consider investing in UK property as your way to become financially independent.

Why not come and join me, Rachel and my other friends and colleagues in our network of like-minded people today?

I hope that you have enjoyed this book and that you are inspired to *Retire Early Retire Wealthy* using UK property investment as the main tool to achieve this.

I look forward to hearing of all your successes

Better still, come and join us, and let us do this together

All the best,

Roly

PEACE
ONE DAY

Rachel and I had always given money to various charities whenever we could and whoever we decided to at any particular time. We did not have a plan and, as such, never really became committed to any one particular charity or charitable cause. That was until we heard Jeremy Gilley speak at an event we attended.

In 1999, filmmaker Jeremy Gilley founded Peace One Day, a non-profit organisation, and in 2001 Peace One Day's efforts were rewarded when the member states of the United Nations unanimously adopted the first ever annual day of global ceasefire and non-violence on ...

21st September – Peace Day – every year

Peace Day is a day for individuals to become part of wide scale community action, as well as a day that provides a window of opportunity for aid organisations to carry out life saving work. Over 4.5 million children have benefited from polio immunisations as a result of Peace Day agreements in Afghanistan between 2007 and 2010.

Peace One Day's objective is to institutionalise Peace Day, 21st September; making it a day that is self-sustaining; an annual day of global unity; a day of intercultural cooperation on a world wide scale.

Rachel and I were so inspired with what Jeremy Gilley and his organisation, Peace One Day, were doing and achieving, that we realised this was something that we really wanted to support.

The work they are doing to promote world peace is so touching and inspirational that we decided to become Patrons and support them with our time and money.

You can support Peace One Day by joining their Global Truce campaign at www.peaceoneday.org

The Patrons are a group of dedicated individuals who ensure that Peace One Day is able to focus on its goals and objectives, by providing strategic and financial support. Patrons also receive a series of exclusive benefits: facilitated networking, exclusive events, media and PR, not to mention the enormous satisfaction that comes from being a part of this worthy cause.

To show my continued support, 25% of the profits from my book and a percentage of the profits from my educational workshops will be given directly to Peace One Day.

If you would like more information on becoming a Patron of Peace One Day please email me at roly@mylifesolutions.co.uk

About the Author

Roly Weaver quit his 'day-job' as a Chartered Civil Engineer at the age of 50 in March 2008 - fulfilling his long standing dream 'to retire early'.

He was able to do this because in 2002, along with his wife Rachel, he started investing in UK property; he bought family houses and rented them out. By March 2008, the income from his property portfolio exceeded his salary. He had become financially independent.

Self taught, using his professional skills, and learning from early mistakes, he designed his own robust rules, systems and processes to become a professional and successful property investor.

Roly's passion is to help people, through his education and mentoring programmes, to accomplish the financial independence he has achieved; so they too, do not have to rely on others to provide a salary or pension for them. They can choose to *'Retire Early Retire Wealthy'*.

To make contact or find out what Roly is currently up to, visit his website at www.mylifesolutions.co.uk

Lightning Source UK Ltd.
Milton Keynes UK
UKOW031119100613

212015UK00008B/348/P